LOOKING BACK ON
THE END OF THE WORLD

SEMIOTEXT(E) FOREIGN AGENTS SERIES
Jim Fleming and Sylvère Lotringer, Editors

LOOKING BACK ON
THE END OF THE WORLD

JEAN BAUDRILLARD
GUNTER GEBAUER
DIETMAR KAMPER
DIETER LENZEN
EDGAR MORIN
GERBURG TREUSCH-DIETER
PAUL VIRILIO
CHRISTOPH WULF

Edited by Dietmar Kamper & Christoph Wulf
Translated by David Antal

SEMIOTEXT(E) FOREIGN AGENTS SERIES

Semiotext(e)
522 Philosophy Hall
Columbia University
New York, New York
10027 USA

Layout and camera-ready copy
prepared by Free University,
Berlin — ZI 7 — SE 3.
Printed in the United States of America.

Table of Contents

Dietmar Kamper and Christoph Wulf

Looking Back on the End of the World

With contributions by Jean Baudrillard, Gunter Gebauer, Dietmar Kamper, Dieter Lenzen, Edgar Morin, Gerburg Treusch-Dieter, Paul Virilio, and Christoph Wulf

The "world" was never more than an image, a regulative idea, a normative concept for planning and implementing a global society. This concept has begun to crumble because of its obvious relationship to the institutions of political power, which know no limits in the use of force if it is necessary. Long veiled and thus precarious, this relationship has become evident. In view of the unjustified differentiation between "First", "Second", "Third", and "Fourth" worlds, it appears that a search for ways to overcome the idea of "one world" is long overdue, a "world" that is characterized by the interplay of the great European powers as it has influenced our historical concepts. Whoever continues to speak of a "united world" today means destruction.

The decline of the great nineteenth-century vision has become more than obvious at the end of the twentieth century. It is not the physical end of the world (though some would tolerate it in order to indulge their obsession with power), it is the imaginary end:

▸ The obsession with the last moment, which everyone wants to experience
▸ The great acceleration of all the trends pointing to the destruction of existing conditions
▸ Current phantasmata based on the seemingly unlimited possibilities for "making" a new human race, possibilities that are becoming openly destructive
▸ The exclusive veneration of methods as such, without regard to their practical outcome
▸ The incapacity to act against the obvious and generally acknowledged trends towards worsening conditions
▸ The aesthetisizing of horrific visions in an attempt to offset the inescapable fate resulting from a global catastrophe

All this seems to indicate the inevitable end of the world.

The articles in this volume deal with the creeping disintegration from the perspective of a second future, pretending that the devastation of the order of world-images has been successfully left behind. The contributers to this volume are intent on to furthering and accelerating the fundamental thought processes involved so as to conceive of an extraterrestrial vantage point and develop a historical type of anthropology and cosmology. The methodology of such endeavors should be adapted to the intrinsic diversity of human existence and the multiformity of the environment in which the human race lives. The outline of the volume reflects the fact that these ideas can only be realized by accepting the concept of universal catastrophe. This view is explored theoretically in three sections:

I. Phantasms of the End of the World (Treusch-Dieter, Gebauer, Baudrillard);
II. Concepts of the End of the World (Wulf, Lenzen); and
III. Beyond Apocalypse (Morin, Kamper, Virilio).

Despite the general consensus among the authors, there remains one question they are unable to agree upon: With the "end of the world" phantasmata in mind, is it more relevant to reduce theoretical considerations and draw more explicitly on the functions of language, or should theory be dealt with in a more explicit way in order to deal better with the complexities of human life and historical development? It was undoubtedly the theoretical foundations of the social and historical sciences as they were conceived in the nineteenth century that fostered the idea of "single world". Those disciplines are affected by the concept of universal catastrophe. Therefore on the one hand, any further theoretical considerations in line with the thoughts of the 19th century are apt to be futile. On the other hand, the simultaneity of decline and transition, of the end and overcoming of our narrow worldview represent a permanent challenge for human thought not to restrict one's thinking to a retrospective view of the end of the world, but rather to do justice to the planet earth with a theory based on new vistas.

I. PHANTASMS OF THE END OF THE WORLD

Gerburg Treusch-Dieter

The Beginning of the End

On the History of Radiation from Plato to Chernobyl

For thousands of years myths of the creation and philosophical discourse have subordinated matter, or the feminine, to form, or the masculine. The radiating spirit
shapes the feminine, that which is passive and conceiving.
This order comes to an end in Chernobyl — matter begins
to radiate. Starting from the concepts of matter, origin,
and abundance, the following observations outline the
link between the classical philosophy of the ancient world
and today's scientific assault on matter.

Abundance?

I have found none, except at two ends of history: today
and long ago. Today's bulletins reported a manifestation
of 1,500 to 2,000 Hiroshima bombs worth of abundance
with which nothing can be done. In a myth long ago there
is a woman's corpse from which an entire world is made:
abundance through immolation. Myths about the immola-

tion of woman abound, but none expresses it as radiantly
as the Babylonian myth of Marduk and Tiamat:

> Tiamat and Marduk, the wisest of the gods, ... began the battle.
> The master spread his net and bound her. He hurled the wicked wind
> in her face. Tiamat opened her mouth to devour it. ... Her belly
> swelled. ... He shot an arrow, which pierced her belly, rending her
> bowels. ... He overcame her, took her life, threw her corpse to the
> ground, and looked down upon it. ... With his merciless weapon he
> split her skull and severed her veins. The north wind bore her blood
> afar. When his fathers saw this, they were glad and rejoiced. ... The
> master, now satisfied, examined the corpse.

From it he makes the world, piece by piece. A creation
of the world that became a model for the Old Testament
as well.

Matter?

Between this ancient creation of the world and its
possible end today, the discussion about matter begins
with classical antiquity, whose radiant legacy is an inextri-
cable part of our minds. Plato celebrates it. Aristotle, the
Stoics, and Plotinus join in. The Church Father Augustine, however, makes this talk the foundation of his
systematic explanation of the creation from nothingness,
an explanation that has become doctrine in Christianity.

Origin?

One thing from which the world arises has already been
mentioned: that corpse. And the other from which
nothing more arises: the energy that passed through
Chernobyl. Both are the effect of splitting. Mythologi-

cally: "With his merciless weapon he split her skull."
Scientifically: "With a device only as large as a table, Otto
Hahn split the atoms of the inherently radioactive
element uranium in his laboratory." Does this not clarify
for both ends of history the age-old question of origin —
which was first, the chicken or the egg? It is the rooster,
the bird that greets the radiant morning, the light. In
myths and fairy tales he loves Tiamat-Goldmarie above
all else. And today he has come so far that "humans can
create every kind of ray they choose by splitting uranium
atoms in order to unleash the immense energies bundled
within them". It is an unleashing for which man once
needed immolation, the time when energies were still
bundled in the blood rather than in the atom. Ever since
Otto Hahn, there are concrete eggs in the countryside,
fast breeders. But at that time, too, the world egg came by
means of the hen only if occasioned by the rooster.

It is becoming clear that matter, origin, and abundance
have to do with the feminine: with matrix, mould,
mattress, manure, must, muck, mumbo jumbo, mass, mud,
cunt and so forth. Or simply mama. This feminine entity is
split by a radiating weapon, a radiating spirit, with this
spirit itself ultimately and finally creating rays in the wake
of the transfer from myth to science. But for the time
being:

A JUST WORD BETWIXT MYTH AND SCIENCE

Between the immolation of yore and Plato's celebration
of matter, there is a passage by the tragedian Aeschylus in
which Orestes is acquitted of matricide. Matricide,
murder of one's mama? Immolation à la Tiamat. The
radiant god Apollo speaks to Orestes:

Hear my just word: Not the mother is the procreator of her child, she only nurtures and carries the sown seed. It is the father who begets, but she keeps the token. . . . For one can be a father without a mother.

A message of light, of enlightenment. True, that does not excuse the matricide historically. But for advanced thinkers like Aeschylus and others of his day, her immolation is transformed into a theorem that makes it superfluous. For why sacrifice someone that does not procreate in the first place? At one time it was the entire world that issued from her. Now it is not even so much as a child. Mama is dichotomized by this radiant message, first into one who cannot conceive; second, into one who is the pawnbroker, the hired mother for the father. In the process birth, too, is negated along with immolation.

PLATO'S IDEAS AND REFLECTIONS

With this dichotomy, Plato comes along with an intellect just as radiant as that of Apollo. The world order he imagines is described in *Timaios*. Over everything there is being, immaterial light. Always remaining the same, it is apprehensible only with the light of reason. Also called the father by Plato, it radiates down, where it produces materially dimmed reflections of its incendiary ideas: the visible world, in view of which even the light of reason does not remain undimmed. But of what does the visible world consist?. It would in principle have to be the mama, if there were one. There is not, though. Instead, there is the wet nurse: matter as a receptacle and recipient that is an "invisible, formless, all-receptive being". It is the hired mother of a ray that is cast back by her as a shadow. For she is bereft of everything that the mother would be as "procreator".

It is empty space; victim that never was; birth that is

not. Air, gap. hole that is also a void in thinking. For it is nothing, has no being, cannot be known. Whoever attempts it anyway is left only with knowledge "without sensory perception", knowledge that is no knowledge. It is an "afterthought" that apprehends deception only: fables, myths, fairy tales in which there lurks what ought not be thought. The bifurcation of the mama into radiated wet nurse and evanescent "procreator" is managed through a ban on thought about and contact, a ban corresponding to the negated immolation. Plato's order only half admits of it, admits of it only as a "contributing cause". The rest remains dark.

ARISTOTLE'S QUINTESSENCE

It is true that Aristotle has much against Plato, but nothing against the above mentioned argument. For him, matter remains what it is for Plato: split. All the same, Aristotle modifies things. According to him, light, radiation, is too far away. Admittedly, it can go ahead and remain up there as ether or quintessence, as matter does down here. But in the visible world something else must happen as well. For who goes by mere reflections of immensely remote ideas? In the visible world form, radiation, must enter things. Here, form must couple with matter, the masculine with the feminine. In no way to the point of lifting the ban on thought and contact, which negates immolation and birth. As "procreator", mama matter remains taboo. But as half or deficiency it shares in being: through form. It imputes the ether, the quintessence of all radiation, of mama matter in the capacity of male sperm so that it can work the humanly possible within her. The rest remains dark.

STOIC SPERM OF LIGHT

The Stoics only seem to lift the ban on thought and contact between form and matter, between male and female, in favor of a single radiating primeval substance. True, the radiation of this primeval substance is immanent from that point on, but as *logos spermatikos*. Ejaculating everywhere it supplies every thing of the visible world with "sperm of light", through which it logically participates in order. In the process matter remains what it is − split. Although the *logos spermatikos* already negates immolation and birth so much that the distinction between "procreator" and wet nurse is almost voided. Because the logos spermatikos seems to integrate itself with the "procreator" by way of the wet nurse. The latter merges completely with the order, radiates with it. The rest remains dark. The more fiery the radiating primeval substance becomes as the center of the earth is approached, the darker the remainder stays.

NEOPLATONIC RADIATION

Stoic worldly-mindedness is turned upside down by Plotinus. Down atop the radiant One from which every-thing emanates. Through a step-by-step flow of sperm, of course, downwards until matter is reached, which at best still corresponds to impure pollution. Pollution: indicator of impotence. That is why matter is compared by Plotinus to the "eunuch", the "man without his member". It shares in order only as a flat surface. Like the manner in which mirrors are angled to focus the sun's rays. The rest remains dark. For as "procreator", matter is purely and simply that which is secreted. It does not exist. That is, matter is no longer present except as a "beggar woman".

Through the immolation of Tiamat, from which the world issued, it is juxtaposed to that abundance as the ultimate deficiency. The ban on thought and contact decreed by Plato, modified by Aristotle, and neutralized by the Stoics is thereby restored when Plotinus completely profaned matter. Completely profaned, it is scarcely the caricature of the feminine any more. Literally, it is a "prank that dissipates". It is ripe for the creation from nothingness.

THE CREATION FROM NOTHINGNESS

The creation from nothingness was fashioned by Augustine from what already existed. The One of Plotinus, personalized into the God of creation, preserves Plato's ideas as thoughts from which − presto! − the whole world suddenly emerges. As a plan that becomes reality only in the course of history. Specifically, when those thoughts, obediently following Aristotle, manifest matter as form. Since the plan of history is a plan of salvation, however, these thoughts are forms in special form. They are the Stoic's *logoi spermatikoi*, which the God of creation radiates or ejaculates into the nothingness of matter. By means of this *semines rationes*, the order established by creation is programmed into matter, or the feminine. But this in such a way that matter, or the feminine, no longer figures as a contributing cause as was still the case with Plato or Aristotle. Like the Stoics, Augustine did hold that matter is big with these *semines rationes*. But as with Plotinus' "beggar woman", it does not give birth.

Matter, or the feminine, can be compared to a hired mother who has been taking the Pill. A contributing cause only for appearances, it is a constraining or catastrophic force confronting the order established by creation; it is "original sin" absolute in which the ban on thought and contact vis-à-vis immolation and birth is repeated — despite the creation from nothingness. This is why matter, or the feminine, must be declared to be the nothing of nothingness. Like the "witch burnings" at the dawn of modern times, this also succeeds with the unfolding of the history of salvation, which ultimately changes into progress. In addition to the intended price entailed in this play underlying the history of salvation has a foreseen as well as an unforeseen price, however. For God, who even in Augustinian thought was not bound to his creation, is abolished by progress. Today we are thus closer than ever to the ancient world and its prehistory.

THE NOTHINGNESS OF CREATION

We are closer than ever to the ancient world and its prehistory because man has, in turn, made himself into God, a transformation thoroughly parallel to the genesis of gods like Marduk, Apollo, and others. There is one difference, though. To be sure, these gods and subsequent spirits already occupied everything perceivable and conceivable in the way of rays, radiation, and exposure to radiation. But for lack of technology, they never progressed beyond the appearance of holding lightening in their fists. Today, that has been managed. Matter and the world have been taken over by technology. At the same time, man no longer has anything in his hands, despite the divine position based on his technologies. In diametric inversion to himself as God, he has been degraded to a worldless point corresponding to an atom, which for him may be the starting point of his world power for the last time.

Is that why uranium is the name of the matter from

which the atom is obtained by fission? A radiant for a
god's name, whether it refers to Uranus or Urania. It is all
the same because mastered matter can no longer be
distinguished from those who have mastered it. By virtue
of the products obtained through the fission of this
material, man as an atom or God erects himself an invisible pantheon of plutonium, neptunium, etc., an edifice
that exceeds every previous one in radiation. Or over-
shadows it. With it, a second accident of the greatest
possible dimensions is assumed; its entire prehistory will
explode in the here and now. While it manifests the
nothingness of creation. Not although but rather because
this prehistory knows of no counterpart to the "peaceful
use" of matter other than catastrophe.

TROUBLE FACTOR: MATTER

The very Tiamat whose immolation in the Babylonian
myth gave rise to the world that may be heading for its
end today, that very Tiamat is a threat to the world made
from her and to her master. A battle ensued, but it was
still a confrontation between master and victim on the
same level. As soon as victim and birth are negated, the
catastrophe to be feared by matter as "procreator"
becomes subversive. Plato, Aristotle, and the Stoics
assume a cyclical annihilation of their world order, an
event always construed as a fatal birth, be it through
earthquake — the self movement of matter — or the fire
in bowels of the earth. For that very reason even Plotinus,
whose world order has no "procreator", does not preclude
the possibility of being swallowed up by matter. Even the
void of the Christian creation described in the Old
Testament contains the Tohuwabohu, in which cloven
Tiamat makes her devastating return: that rest of her

which remained dark, which still cannot be discounted even when nuclear fission is involved. For as stated by the supervisor of the Chernobyl construction crew (quite against all orders): "The split atom, too, is treacherous, even if we use it for peaceful purposes." Matter is "residual risk" to the extent that it is used up in its capacity as residual. By means of atomization.

Missing Senses

Matter has dematerialized. In the accounts of Chernobyl, it is "what is imperceptible by hands, eyes, and ears". It, the radioactive radiation, cannot even be "sensed". Is it as if man has no sensory organ for something that he himself produced? Undoubtedly, it is possible if he does not produce one, too, if he rationalizes it away not despite but because of his radiant ideas, forms, *logoi spermatikoi*, *semines rationes*, emanations, and emissions. But does not the effect of this radiant legacy — that matter for its part now radiates back — make it plausible that man would very likely possess a sensory organ for matter's dematerialization if he had he not already abolished it back in the days of Plato? For by means of a ban on thinking and contact with respect to immolation and birth, he declared matter to be an "invisible" and "formless" entity. But if this ban on thinking and contact remained in effect up to the dematerialization of matter, then the opposite question suggests itself: that of whether nuclear fission is not the effect of this abolished, this historically unco-developed organ? An effect resulting from the negation of matter, which implies matter's reduction to nothingness.

FALLOUT

Amazingly, the energy that flowed through Chernobyl is radiating back in a way that eclipses history's customary dialectic of "peaceful use" and catastrophe. True, on one hand it went downwards into the concrete. That represents the existing, historically developed senses in that they take recourse for the umpteenth time to the catastrophe metaphors of fatal birth. Energy was discharged as radioactive "brew", "plug", and "nuggets". As aborted tissue. On the other hand, the senses for the fallout upwards were absent. Accordingly, dematerialized matter radiates back in just the same way, despite catastrophe, as if it were a matter of its "peaceful use". As if matter were the nonexisting, all pervasive entity that is formless and invisible.

One could have been passed over this dematerialized matter "with inward and outward silence" as has always been done if this radiating were not turned in on itself. An inversion that is indescribable, although it is described with the words "intangible danger", and "creeping epidemic". With this radiation that is turned in on itself, the customary historical dialectic of "peaceful use" and catastrophe is eclipsed to the same degree that it no longer contaminates, no longer defiles anything. Radiantly and cleanly, it manifests what is written of matter that has been cleansed of itself as "procreator": it brings forth nothing, lets everything decay.

MATTER IN REVERSE GEAR

The body's female zones — the skin, mouth, and intestines — are where "radiation sickness" begins, which is nothing other than death as the runaway growth of living tissue. Cancer. The forms, the fact that one can observe matter in reverse gear. It invades the body from sources that have been declared to be the paragon of the peaceful. Starting with grass, herbs, and milk. With pregnant women being the most endangered. That is precisely why it is no coincidence that the intention is to replace birth by means of gene technology and reproduction technology at the very moment that the abundance of matter becomes the ultimate defect, becomes cancer in reverse gear. Vitrofertilization is the way there. With vitrofertilization the dichotomy of the feminine into "procreator" and wet nurse becomes reality once and for all in that it combines the contributor of the egg and the hired mother. Simultaneously, this customary historical dialectic will also be eclipsed by it in that it turns the beginning of life in on itself. For the time being it still takes place in live beings or in the feminine. But by being transferred from the feminine to the test tube, by being given over to the splitting of cellular nuclei, its paradigm is vitrofertilization from now on.

Of course, gene and reproduction technology, too, have a radiant message, which it is proclaiming with the cockcrow of enlightenment, which is supposed to acquit it of matricide. Its legitimation is the early recognition of hereditary damage, which, however, is nothing other than the long-term effect of the humanly produced reversal of matter. It is obvious that our historically developed senses would have to go by their own breakdown if it is not to be too late to recognize the fallout that they produce on account of the radiant legacy of the ancient world and its prehistory.

Gunter Gebauer

The Place of Beginning and End

Caves and Their Systems of Symbols

The first art created by the human race developed from the rhythms of the hands, from even movements that fashioned tools from stones. The first forms were groped for, found, seized upon, then executed with increasing assurance and spread to widely scattered areas of Europe as representational conventions for a limited array of copies. Paleolithic art reaches its peak in large pictorial ensembles of increasingly rich and exquisitely decorated caves and dies out after a fundamental climatic change — a considerable warming of the earth — as man settles down in permanent village communities. Human culture starts from that point. It will introduce farming, animal husbandry, technologies, writing, and social organizations. By comparison, cave art appears to be a forgotten period, lost, without influence on later development. Unlike this common interpretation, the view presented here maintains that the end of paleolithic art left a profound void in the human race's memory.

For an immense period of time prehistoric people were

involved in working out their system of symbols. The paleolithic period lasted from 30,000 to 8,000 B. C., time enough to make its imprint on human heritage. Cave art is the first formulation of a human language of form; its inception is the foundation of *all* systems of symbols and intellectual constructs. The extinction of paleolithic culture was the end of the man's first world, an irretrievable loss. We are thus bereft of knowledge about our beginnings, which are inscribed into our lives and which are still present regardless of the forms subsequent cultures may have assumed. The adoption of a settled life was a step forward, but in the development of the human race it was also a breach that has led to irreversible amnesia concerning our origins and that has left an uncontrolled source of longing.

The first pictorial forms were made in free space created by autonomic rhythms: even movements of the hand, uniformly executed, many individuals repeating the same operations the same way over and over, controlling them with their eyes. The rhythms leave imprints on stone tools. The fingers of the hands are freed, they are passed over the surfaces of clay and stone and continue the rhythms. In the surfaces they leave traces that solidify into outlines and are perceived as such. The hand produces forms that correspond to the chance characteristics of the material, of etching, of scratching, and of striking but that at the same time also aim at a precisely defined function of the tool being made, that of craft work and killing.

The muscles of the hand doing the striking, the eye controlling the emerging shapes, and the ear hearing the tempo of the movements are coordinated with each other and enter into the "socializing" rhythm that unites the group of people working together. The shaping activity of the liberated hand expands the coordination of seeing and gripping to include the dimension of speech, for the imaginative creations born of their play do not yet speak for themselves; words must be used to help indentify them. The expressive capacity of verbal speech, which is already present at this point, is "translated" into pictorial representations. The experiences of hand-eyecoordination, one of the great achievements setting homo sapiens apart from all their ancestors, become exteriorized in paleolithic art, that is, given expression through the objects depicted.

The essence of cave art and its emergence is not so much the formal mastery, elegance, and eloquence that it is to gain in later stylistic epochs as it is the transition represented by this exteriorization. After the development of speech, the slow appearance of reflective thinking enters a new stage with pictorial representation. Cave art furthered a development that had been initiated by speech — the integration of the human being into a definite space, something that had originated in the search for security and a largely homogeneous view of the world that paleolithic people had in common. This drive is rooted in genetically conditioned behavior of animals, in retreat, in the search for the nest and the lair in the earth. Transposed into symbols, however, something quite different arises — a space in the earth with features of the sacred and a medium of man's expression of himself.

The freeing of the hands from the task of providing locomotion, their assimilation into the rhythm of other movements, which are then bound only by speech, can be regarded as a kind of "play". It is play bound by few rules, if any, play shaped only by the physical regularity of speech and its conventions of interpretation, a ludic flow state of humans woven into a community of economic, technological, and sexual relationships. Very gradually the flow of the hand movements takes on the contours of objects, like the written characters of a text. The playing of the hands becomes play with language, the shaping of words in a text. In the touching, in the feeling of the other bodies, in the sensitive and keenly perceptive contact between one's own fingers and the microzones of the other body, its hair, and its skin, human affectivity towards the other is awakened. The scratching and engraving of human shapes into resistant, hard materials also bespeaks affective relations to that which is being portrayed. Instead of relating trivialities to us, the flow of the play leads us to important, fundamental attidudes of the community in which it is developed. In this sense, it is "deep play": By engaging in this play a community takes a risk, for in that play it develops something that lies at its core. In this play, paleolithic man indicates and accepts his physical aspect. It contains his view of himself and of others. In a certain regard the significance of the human being is tied to the play with invented ideographical forms. This dimension gives cave art its splendor, its magnificence, and its richness.

Play, seriousness, and affectivity enter into cave pictures all at once. The objects represented in the earliest stages — the human sexual organs — have these three features and are eminently physical in nature: circular vulvas engraved in stone and simple pairs of lines signifying the male member. The primordial play conceives a world of gender. The portrayal of the sexual organs is abstract and stylized. They pass through an evolution of artistic forms, remaining idealizing signs. There is no indication of sexual activity; the representations are influenced by affect and are classificational signs. They are combined with and likened to other signs. The differences between the sexes are brought out on the purely physical level in a manner as idealizing as it is affective and are accentuated by means of animal analogies. But the contextual use of these symbols tends to suggest their complementary nature.

Thus arises a system of symbols that is articulated but at the same time the opposite of articulated; it is, in other words, analogous to fluid transitions that cannot be circumscribed. The vulva does not symbolize "woman" as opposed to "man" but rather stresses the sexual aspect of woman and relates it to other features, which are developed by means of animal series. Above and beyond all differences, the female and male symbols are combined according to certain schemes whose meaning is unclear.

These peculiarities are the "principles" of the first human system of symbols. The most important means of expression are the metaphorical relationship. The metaphor focuses on features in nature and relates them to what is human, to what is individual, and to the group. In addition to animals, the earth serves as a reservoir of metaphors. The cave itself, which contains and preserves the symbols, is a metaphor for the organized world depicted in it. Like other metaphors, it is an idealization and enhancement: the shelter, the silent darkness, the immutable ecology, the curvatures, the crevices and passageways. It is the perfect interior, directed against the chaos outside. The bowels of the earth are an idealized world to which all symbolic representations of paleolithic man refer. The cave is nature with her randomness, but it is *selected* nature, in which the natural geologic, contingent, formations of niches, passageways, and walls were given notional shape through abstract symbolism and interpretation. Inside the earth the community establishes its order of life, encoding it in signs; it is more than a utopia.

It is at once an expression of the existing human being. This is recognized by the fact that *man*, and nothing else, is the "scale" of this order.

How man enters into the world of the cave will be shown shortly. Consider one other thought first, though. The human race set itself apart from animality by changing animals into masks as it were. What man almost manages to achieve but not quite, is the insight into his face. Man conceals it or still refrains from giving himself one. He has, so to speak, not yet exposed it. The relationships within the group, to the other, are not yet conveyed through the expressive capacity of the face.

Paleolithic art organizes relationships between the members of a community according to sexual features, to physical characteristics, which are metaphorically connoted on animals, and to a third entity to which attention will be turned shortly: the hands. The female sexual symbols, for example, appear together with certain animals but are also likened to wounds. Physical similarity with certain injuries and the impression of spurting blood may play a role in this analogy. What becomes clear, however, is the high degree of artificiality characterizing this world of women. On one hand, it is marked by signs denoting vulnerability and peril; on the other hand, it is precisely the sheltering space, the cave, that takes on clearly female traits. The symbolism unites two openings that occur to us as being quite different: the opening that ultimately means the loss of life and the opening that represents access to a protective interior. Features of the female body are stylized and integrated into a symbolic context; several symbolic levels are superimposed upon the physical.

The body is the foundation of paleolithic ideography. Now cave painters go about depicting their hands on sub-

terranean walls in the most exact manner there is, by
holding them agoinst the rock surface and covering them
with pigment. In irregular fields of color one finds the so-
called negatives of hands, exact copies of the *real* hand,
the surfaces that were covered by the hand and thus not
painted over.

The tools that paved the way to ideography, the
"writing" hands, get "written" themselves. It is not simply
the actual hands that appear in the images but the hands
in self-reflection. Certain places in the caves are reserved
for them − in the vicinity of the entrance; above passageways, especially niches; in combination with other signs,
including other hands. The cave of Gargas has whole
compositions of hands, sixty-four in all − an artistically
arranged, composite world of hands. In these images, one
can see a key to paleolithic ideography. The symbolism
emanates from the human body. With his body, man
enters into his system of symbols, serving it simultaneously as a standard for representation, as a module, and
is himself seized upon by the symbols and transformed
into signs.

The entire artificial, complex world of symbols lacks
one characteristic that we take for granted − it describes
no situations. Its pictures become more and more precise,
realistic, but they do not narrate, they show no development, no chronological sequence, neither beginning nor
end. It remains encapsulated in its cave even though it
evokes distant things. It is unable to indicate any goals. It
is bonded to the only situation it knows: the situation on
hand, that of the cave as a kind of inner landscape, a
natural hiding place, a controlled microecology with areas
imbued with human-like qualities: the central ones as
female, the remote ones as male. For our eyes, it is a
terminus; one cannot imagine a space that came before or

after it. It symbolizes both the beginning and end of the world.

For paleolithic man, the cave is a place of self-encounter. In it, he acquires a self and construes a world on his scale. The cave is the place of initial identification and, closely linked with that, of initial societal differentiation. But it is the counterprinciple to the dynamics of the individual and society, for in the cave nothing can be changed. Not until man settles down to live in village communities and starts to use more advanced technologies does human development begin to progress.

The cave does not represent reality as it exists aboveground. From this comes the peculiar character of paleolithic drawings as play. The cave is different; its landscape does not represent the external conditions of the earth but rather the *inner* state of man. The cave allows one to take a step back from experience. Humans become animals; they are manifested *differently* without *becoming different*. Man gives himself with the traits of the magnificent (G. Bataille) while his existence on earth is the most perilous of all. The fascinating thing about the human being is the animal-like features; the most fascinating thing about the animal, the human-like features.

The world of the cave, even as a partial inversion of the world that exists aboveground, expresses an ordering of experience. In that sense it resembles other "deep plays". The vulva, the hand, the wound, the cave: the fact that analogies are made between these very different spheres reveals a specific way of organizing experiences into a specific schematic pattern.

The relationships between the members of a group are recorded in the sites of the caves and the material to which they are indissolubly tied. The individual can recognize himself and the others in it again. In a certain way, the relationships to the other are themselves part of the cave, too. They are encased within them and cannot be removed.

In the paleolithic cave man finds himself face to face with pictures of himself and his position in relation to the others. The rock walls are his projection area. He reads in them what he is. This has nothing to do with truth; rather, it has to do with the construction of something new, of something that is not there: with his self, his inner being, and with the relationships between individuals. To allow this to emerge, it needs the protection of a powerful other inner being, a stable, unchanging sanctuary that opens to the outside. The cave is not simply a likeness; rather, it produces a place that favors for the exteriorization of human relations. Like every genuine myth, Plato's cave myth has a core relating to actual development. Long after leaving the caves, he still sees danger in them. Caves, precisely because of their pictures, threaten to captivate and hold those who descend into them. In the cradle of the cave, one finds one's own image. The fascinating images virtually defy the effort to tear oneself away from contemplating them. In this sense the cave has never been abandoned once and for all. Our gaze is still on the rock surfaces, on the brilliantly colored, consummate shadow in which man recognizes himself again – or makes himself.

Our inner being has its origin in the topography of caves. It is also related to a *place*, a specific ecology. That inner being's faculty of imagination, its visions of paradise are focused on finding a place where it can unfold. Paradise remains the spatial vision of a place whose space and time is dominated by humans.

In the search of the ideal place, the earth's interior plays the lead role. The earth gives the scope for a natural kind of symbolism. Her center was interpreted as being feminine in paleolithic times. The departure from the bowels of the earth was prepared by so-called mobile art. The subterranean shrines are abandoned; small movable objects symbolize, in the most confined of spaces, portable, adjustable religious symbols, the most important ones ever represented in the cave up to that time. The departure from the bowels of the earth destroys the natural symbolism of religious signs. The essential element of ideography was the earth's interior with its special ecology and topography — the darkness, the crevice, the shelter, the dome, the entrance. This art seems to be rooted in these things as in fertile soil. To that extent, the abandonment of the caves is destructive.

Our imagination remains captive in the cave. We do, in fact, repeatedly seek out the cave in a different form. In one way or another, all our notions of paradise are linked with situations of the cave.

Jean Baudrillard

The Anorexic Ruins

In the effort to manage crisis, it has become apparent
that growth has ended and that we have entered a field
whose consequences are unpredictable.

We are no longer in a state of growth; we are in a state
of excess. We are living in a society of excrescence, meaning that which incessantly develops without being meas-
urable against its own objectives. The boil is growing out
of control, recklessly at cross purposes with itself, its
impacts multiplying as the causes disintegrate. That is
leading to enormous congestion of the systems, to their
deregulation through hypertely, through an excess of func-
tionality, through virtual satiation. This process can be
compared best with cancerous metastases – conditions in
which a body's organic rules of the game are lost, en-
abling such a formation of cells to manifest its invincible
and fatal vitality, partially leading it to stop obeying its
own genetic commands, and finally to grow rampantly
instead of following an organized pattern of development.

It is no longer a matter of a critical process; crisis is
functional. It is always a matter of causality, of imbalance
between causes and effects, and is (or indeed is not)

resolved in a new arrangement of causes. As far as we are concerned, however, it is the causes that are obliterated and that become indecipherable by making way for an intensification of the process in a void.

As long as there is contradiction and dysfunction in a system, as long as the known laws governing its functioning are disobeyed, there is no great problem since there is still the possibility of reaching a solution by overextending. What is worse − bordering more on a catastrophe than on a crisis − is when the system overextends itself, when it has already left its own goals behind and thereby no longer has any remedies at hand. A lack is never dramatic; it is satiation that is disastrous, for it simultaneously leads to lockjaw and inertia.

I am amazed by the obesity of all current systems, this incarnation of evil, as Susan Sontag said of cancer, that is represented by our means of communication, memory, storage, production, and destruction, means that have been expanded and overburdened so much that their uselessness is a foregone conclusion. It is not we ourselves who have put an end to their utility in theory; the system itself has liquidated it through overproduction. So many things are being manufactured and piled up that they will simply never find more time to serve anyone (and that is naturally extremely welcome in the case of nuclear weapons, for the obesity of the systems of destruction is the only thing that protects us from their use). So many messages and signals have been produced and transmitted that they will never find the time to acquire any meaning. Fortunately so for us! Fortunately, we ignore 99 % of all information, 99 % of the products. The tiny amount that we nevertheless absorb already subjects us to perpetual electrocution.

There is something particularly disgusting about this

atrocious uselessness, however. It is the disgust for a world that is growing, accumulating, sprawling, sliding into hypertrophy, a world that cannot manage to give birth. All these memories, all these archives, all this documentation that do not give birth to a single idea, all these plans, programs, and decisions that do not lead to a single event, all these refined and sophisticated weapons that do not lead to any war!

This satiation has nothing to do with the excess of which Bataille spoke and which all societies have managed to produce and destroy in useless and wasteful exhaustion. We no longer know how we can possibly use up all these accumulated things, we no longer even know what they are for. All we know any more is their awkward or brutal decompensation — every factor of acceleration and concentration is like a factor bringing us closer to the point of inertia. What we call crisis is only a presentiment of that point.

This principle of satiation and inertia can be read as the desolation of time, of the body, of the land. In the human order there is no longer an ideal principle governing these things. What remains is concentrated, satiated, miniaturized effects. This body, our body, appears only as nonessential, basically as useless in its size, in its multiplicity, and in the complexity of its organs, its materiality, and its functions, what with being everything concentrated today in the head and in the genetic formula that alone, in turn, encompasses the operational definition of being. The land, the giant geographic country, seems to be a desolated body whose size is completely unnecessary (and to cross it might be boring) as soon as all events become concentrated in the towns, which for their part are, in turn, heading for reduction to a few miniaturized, salient places. And time? What should one say about this copious free time we are left with, this excess of time that has surrounded us like blurry terrain, like a long useless dimension, ever since the instantaneousness of communication miniaturized our exchange into a sequence of moments?

If one really thinks about it, this dual process of lockjaw and inertia, of accelerating in a vacuum and outdoing production while lacking social inputs and goals, reflects the increase in visibility where there is nothing to see, reflects the dual aspect with which we describe crisis today: inflation and unemployment. But this analysis in terms of inflation and unemployment is conventional and deceptive because it puts everything on the same socioeconomic plane. As we know, conventional inflation and traditional unemployment are variables integrated into the equation of growth. At that level there is no crisis at all − it is a matter of anomic processes, and anomie represents the shadow of organizational solidarity. As such, anomie is not disturbing at all. What is disturbing, however, is anomaly. We are thus in the sphere of the anomalous. Anomaly is not a clear symptom; it is a peculiar sign of weakness, a transgression against a secret, unfamiliar rule of the game. It may be an excess of finality, but we do know that exactly. Something escapes us; we escape ourselves in a process of no return, we have missed a certain point for turning back, a certain point of the contradiction in things, and have entered a universe of noncontradiction alive, of blind rapture, of ecstasy, of amazement about the irreversible processes that nevertheless have no direction at all.

Look at money. Inflation, that is the crisis, agreed. But something else is far more disturbing or, better, more astounding: the mass of floating money globally encircling the earth. It is the only really artificial satellite. Money has become a pure artefact, an artefact of a celestial movement, of a momentary exchangeability. Money has finally found its proper place, one far more unusual than in the stock exchange: the earth orbit, in which it rises and falls like an artificial sun.

Unemployment, agreed. But it is known that it, too, has changed its meaning. It is no longer a strategy of capital (the reserve army) and, vice versa, it no longer represents a critical element within the game of social relations. It has long since been invalidated as a warning signal and has had to make way for unprecedented reversals. What, then, constitutes unemployment today? It, too, represents a kind of artificial satellite, a satellite of inertia, a mass that is loaded not even with negative electricity but rather with static electricity, an ever greater break-up of society, which is ossifying, losing momentum through inertia, and in extreme cases itself becoming a museum object in the German factories of illusions. It bears witness to this increasing inertia in all spheres behind the acceleration of circular flows and exchange. As the movement spins out of control like this, something in each one of us slows down until it vanishes from circulation. An inversion has taken place: all society begins to gravitate around this point of inertia. Paul Virilio has very correctly called it "polar inertia". It is as if the poles of our world were converging, and this merciless short circuit manifests both overproduction *and* the exhaustion of potential energies at the same time. It is no longer a matter of crisis but of disaster, a catastrophe in slow motion.

The real crisis lies in the fact that policies no longer permit this dual political game of hope and metaphorical promise. The pole of reckoning, dénouement, and apocalypse (in the good and the bad sense of the word), which we had been able to postpone until the infiniteness of the

Day of Judgment, this pole has come infinitely closer, and one could join Canetti in saying that we have already passed it unawares and now find ourselves in the situation of having overextended our own finalities, of having short-circuited our own perspectives, and of already being in the hereafter, that is, without horizon and without hope.

Look at the two great events: [the advent of] nuclear power and revolution. It is utterly pointless to hope for the one or fear the other since both have already occurred. Everything has already been liberated, changed, undermined; what more do you want? It is useless to hope: things are there; born or stillborn, they are there, done. Imagination reigns; enlightenment and intelligence reign. We are already experiencing or soon will experience the perfection of the societal. Everything is there. The heavens have come down to earth. We sense the fatal taste of material paradise. It drives one to despair, but what should one do? *No future.*

Nevertheless, do not panic. Everything has already become nuclear, faraway, vaporized. The explosion has already occurred; the bomb is only a metaphor now. What more do you want? Everything has already been wiped off the map. It is useless to dream: the *clash* has gently taken place everywhere.

The last bomb, the one no one speaks about, is the bomb that is not content to strew things in space but would strew them in time. The temporal bomb. Where it explodes, everything is suddenly blown into the past; and the greater the bomb's capacity, the further into the past they go. Look around: this explosion has already occurred. In an amnesic world like ours, everything living is projected into the past as though things had been over-hastily plunged into a dimension in which the only meaning they acquire is that wrested from time by a final revolution. That is the real bomb, the bomb that immobilizes things in eerie retrogression.

* * *

The Berlin Wall is a good example of this. Suddenly, I stand before it without perceiving myself. [It has] a long series of graffiti running from one end to the other like those in the New York subway, like the decal of the West. All at once I have lost the historical imagination of this wall, of this divided city, divided like a head divided into two hemispheres by an artificial scalpel. The adjacent buildings bear charred traces of a hot history - while the cold history feeds on cold, transparent signs that drive the imagination to despair (and the graffiti, too, are cold signs — the only humorous signs are the rabbits scurrying around between the barbed wire entanglements of no-man's land).

It is impossible to recapture the tremor of terror. Everything is insignificant — here, at the pinnacle of history self-exposed by its violence, everything is eerily quiet like an abandoned November field. Every other abandoned urban zone offers the same spectacle. The most amazing thing is that history is being antiquated as vague terrain. One can remember it like some nightmare, that is, like fulfilling a desire, but the signs have long since become a true battlefield. They are the true conductors of lethal energy, the electrodes of electrocution. Today, it is the circular flows that burn, those of the head, those of the sensorial and beloved machines that we ourselves are. It is no longer the buildings that go up in flames and the cities that collapse; it is the Hertzian relays of our memories that crackle.

I view this wall with astonishment, and I no longer

manage to remember anything. It is no different with me than it will be with those who in two thousand years might view this wall, which by that time will have only historical significance for them. By closing my mind's eye, I can see it like Christo's wall, that gigantic curtain of material stretched across the hills of California. . . . Whence this passion for unrolling bandages, walls — here, for example, the historical concrete closure; elsewhere, the magnetic strips? Whence among scientists, for example, this contrived development of chromosome chains or DNA spirals? Things are packaged in their own innermost reaches, in their inner coils, and this imbroglio need not be untangled. Here, the labyrinth of a city and the Gordian knot of history are destroyed at the same time in one stroke by a murderous incision.

* * *

The Day After

The same is true of this film, which would have to instill a salutary terror. The bomb deters; one must deter the bomb. Hence, I fail to see or imagine anything in the course of this film. Its giant images deceive the eye and greatly disturb me. I feel here neither the horror nor the charm of nuclear power but rather the horror and the charm of the ice age; not the suspense and not the final flash.

Is this film bad (certainly), or is it not more likely that all this is unimaginable? In the realm of our imagination, is the nuclear clash not a total event without a day after whereas in the film it leads simply to a regression of the human species? But we know that already; we have just been through it. We dream of something that would no longer have any place within the human order. Where would the earth get air if we were no longer around? In a word, we are dreaming of our disappearance. We dream of looking at the world in a state of formal cruelty, in its inhuman purity (which is not a natural state at all but rather, quite the contrary, the world with a human face).

The dismaying thing about the bomb, about nuclear power, is something quite similar. It has to cover the human with a glacis and put an end to our sentimental delirium of the world. It has to lead us back to a pure geology of the elements and events.

Can that be made into pictorial metaphors? It is by no means certain that the possibility of conjuring up such a thing is not just as remote as that of conjuring up the genetic code and our biomolecular fate, that other dimension of nuclear power. That does not touch us, or no longer touches us — which proves that we are already contaminated. Intellectually, this has all occurred a thousand times already, and all the catastrophe is now is a kind of painted ribbon. The coarse projection into a film is only a diversion from the nuclearization of everyday life. Better yet, this film itself *is* our catastrophe. It does not represent our catastrophe, it does not allow it to be dreamt. On the contrary, it says that the catastrophe is already there, that it has already occurred *because the very idea of the catastrophe is impossible.*

The Berlin Wall embodies the absolute character of the Cold War and its ambiguity. The graffiti covering the Wall do equivocal homage to that war by aestheticizing it — like a dog or a slave would use flowers to braid the whip that beats them. It is no accident when Moretti can undertake to reproduce them life-size with the participation of the protagonists of the Wall itself, the residents of Kreuzberg. The graffiti were painted with the colors of dissidence, this indulgent, intellectual scenario of the Cold War in a context that is disintegrating more and more as a context. Someday one will have to denounce this mystification of dissidence in which western intellectuals come to shudder at the Wall out of cerebral shame and cheaply formulate an aesthetic of human rights, a sentimental aesthetic of the gulag. In its way, the Wall translates the end of this clear division between good and evil. Like many a monument, it has become a nostalgic sign of this division, and like many an event all it is able to do any more is express the nostalgia of history, just as many a furor is able to express only nostalgia of that fury. All the worse if things have already changed — one cannot keep weeping over an anorexic history, over the anorexic ruins.

* * *

We know about the social and political void preceding election day. Every initiative is postponed, the bets are made, *rien ne va plus*, society is already frostbitten in advance. It is pure simulation, incidentally, for the electoral outcome itself does not matter in the least. Every political power tries hard to freeze society through this electoral suspense, this ecstasy of the ballot or survey. One gets the impression that the approach of the year 2000 suffices to make the political societies rigidify retrospectively in the same way. Since the beginning of the 1980s, a timeless area has emerged that will survive by deterrence, like crisis has already done, out of fear that something too significant could happen. If it were possible, one would suspend time before this anniversary of the millennium arrives (the year 2000 will not take place). It is true that this is a metaphor, but it is one that concerns us. What I mean is that this stopping of time, this fear of the millennium and of this whole metaphysical or historical convulsion that is symbolized by the approach of the next millennium has long since occurred. The fear is manifested in the collective indifference to the political development of societies — a kind of end to the efforts made in the previous century without anyone really having any premonition of anything else. And the euphoria of the new information society is not succeeding at masking this mental recession into indifference, this retardation of time as it approaches its end.

Thus, aspects of this intellectual recession are the point at issue. As in the film *2001*, we are journeying into space, with the computer monitoring us. The information, communication, etc., keep the social body in a state of perfect survival, ensuring that all vital functions continue: circulation, breathing, metabolism, heart tone, cell regeneration — just as the computer does it with the biophysiological functions of the voyagers in *2001*. Quite simply, there is no life any longer. Nor is there any in our societies. In a certain way there is no life any more, but the information and the vital functions continue. When the time has passed, the passengers must certainly awaken unless the computer, acting on some vengeful or evil impulse, were really to disconnect them so that they never reach their destination. So it is with us as well. Thus far the risk of being disconnected from the vital functions is still small, but we are already more or less disconnected from our history and thus also from its destination. That means, then, that time can slow as it nears its end and that the year 2000, in a certain way, will not take place.

* * *

Orwell had it easy when fixing 1984 as the crucial point. What we are condemned to may be, after time itself has unfolded, the disappearance of time in the instantaneousness of action. That is the price of change. In the exaltation of uninterrupted circulation and incessant up-to-dateness, societies lose the thread of their development. It is just as with speed: acceleration leads to the loss of direction. The hysteria of change conceals the hysteresis of processes, especially that of the historical process, which in truth does not discontinue but rather extends and persists through inertia and thus seems quite tranquil in its own course. The meters measuring history have come to a standstill in the east with communism; in the west, with a "liberal" society discomfited by its own excess. Under such circumstances there is no longer any stake in original political strategies. The one who enters the scene just when the meters stop stands a good chance of remaining at that point and letting history idle.

We are only inferior imitators. The events, the discoveries, the essential visions are those of the years from 1920 to 1930. We live now only as wearied explainers of that furious epoch, in which all the invention of modernism (even the prescient premonition of its end) came about in a language that still attached importance to magnificence in style. The maximum in intensity lies behind us; the minimum in passion and intellectual inspiration lie before us. As in a general entropic movement of the century, the initial energy is disintegrating ponderously into ever more refined ramifications of structural, pictorial, ideological, linguistic, psychoanalytic upheavals – the ultimate configuration, that of "postmodernism", undoubtedly characterizes the most degenerated, most artificial, and most eclectic phase – a fetishism of picking out and adopting all the significant little bits and pieces,

all the idols, and the purest signs that preceded this fetishism.

Even the great reflection of the 1960s and 1970s, observed from a little distance, will have been only an
episode in the involutionary course of the century, but an
omen nevertheless. Surprise could spring only from a new
event, but we know nothing of that, for the archive and
the analysis of all past events will never convey a future
event to us. Postmodernism functions via this unpre-
dictability and by means of this lack of events.

Postmodernism is the simultaneity of the destruction of
previous values and their reconstruction. It is restoration
in distortion. In concepts of time, the point at issue is the
end of final calculations, of the movement of the (extra-
ordinarily modern) transcendence in favor of "telenomic"
estimates, of the development in concepts of retroaction.
Here everything is retroactive, feedback, including (and
especially) information. For perhaps information, unlike
the view that one has of it, marks only the *retrospective*
omnipotence of our technologies, that is, an infinite
possibility of dealing with the *given facts*. But this
concerns only given facts and not the chance of a new
vision. With it, we will enter the age of exhaustive representation, i. e., of exhaustion as well. Generalized interac-
tion puts an end to special action. A generalized interface
puts an end to the challenge, passion, and rivalry of
peoples.

* * *

Collectively and individually, the phase of the heroic is
past and is making way for a phase of balance, which is
also the phase of crisis since balance is always critical by
definition, albeit without serious consequences. The

pointer oscillates only around a hypothetical center, a statistical mean. Oscillations no longer result in inversions since the system no longer has a gravitational center. The crisis of '29, which was a real catastrophe, cannot happen again today. It has been supplanted by a perpetual simulation of crisis. Unlike a society's heroic or intrinsic values, the simulated, synthetic values (see Reagan) that have taken their place no longer threaten to collapse. Their own weight no longer threatens to result in their loss. They float or, like money, move like a coiling snake.

And that is how we do it in our lives. We get ahead, we move along by oscillating around a hypothetical line of balance, far from fateful deviations.

* * *

This concludes the attempt at imagining a rupture. We are settling into a *modus vivendi* without illusion, without bitterness, and without violence. The issue is not resignation since there is no alternative phantasm. That is just the way it is; that is the way of life. *Modus vivendi:* the concept says exactly what is meant. One comes to an agreement, an arrangement with the situation; reciprocal indifference is negotiated. And the same goes for the general political cycle — a lethargic relationship between the masses and power. One refuses to change the form that it assumes, for any alternative illusion is dead. The political relation consists in the same conjugal neurosis in which a couple or subsequent generations live vis-a-vis preceding ones. The price to be paid is a weak identity, weak intensity, low standard, an air-conditioned intelligence that tries to avoid passing the threshold of a breach.

Fulfillment, achievement, self-expression, free enterprise: the new values have the wind at their backs. Not to mention religion, to which people are returning as if to fantastical terrain. This was already true of philosophy earlier. One wonders what was able to extinguish the impacts of two centuries of critical and subversive spirit so quickly. Class violence has ended, sexual liberation has ended. Marx and Freud: old libertarians and archaic culture. Everything that was swept away in '68 is now restored in — alas! — total eclecticism. That is the change.

The softening of thinking began with ideology of candor, the New Philosophers. It continued with the New Romanticists. Then came the revival of philosophy in general, followed by the enthusiasm for entrepreneurship and new tasks. The social "naturalism" of neoliberalism. Lifted values are emerging everywhere again, a moving dynamism, a childish religiosity in which love, too, is resprouting at the surface. For the horde it is a way to draw the ranks in again at the moment of their greatest dispersion.

* * *

Human rights, dissidence, antiracism, the antinuclear movement, and the environment are gentle ideologies. They are easy, *post coitum historicum*, after the orgy; ideology for an agreeable generation — the children of crisis, who are acquainted with neither hard ideologies nor radical philosophies. They are the ideology of a neoromantic and politically neosentimental generation that is rediscovering love, selflessness, togetherness, international compassion, and the individual tremolo. Effusion, solidarity, cosmopolitan emotivity and multimedia pathos: they are all feeble values long ago tried out by the other Marxist-Freudian generation (as well as by a Rimbaldian, Jarrian, and situationistic generation). It is a new generation, one of children ruined by crisis, whereas the preceding generation was the one of children cursed by history. These young romanticists, these fashionable, power-hungry, sentimental ones are rediscovering the poetic prose of the heart while at the same time treading the path of economic involvement. For they are contemporaries of the new entrepreneurs, who, in turn, are splendid media animals. Transcendental and publicly marketable idealism. Close to the money, the fads, the high-powered careers, to all the things still denounced by the hard generations. At bottom a soft lack of morals and a sensuousness. A soft ambition as well, that of a generation that has already succeeded in everything, that already has everything, that practices solidarity with the greatest of ease, that bears neither the stigma of class misfortune nor the stigma of being cursed by capital. The members of this generation go about their business casually. They are European yuppies.

* * *

There is a tendency for the present culture to develop new health, to adopt a virtue, an intellectual moral, to relink itself to the instructive pursuit of science, history, epistemology, and democracy. The gap opened by the 1960s and 1970s is closing again; each person is arming himself for an operational perspective that is only a defensively-minded reaction against the approaching year 2000. The long blackmail with crisis has begun, intellectually as well, the centration, the recentration, the end of centrifugal passions.

There is a decline of luxurious thinking, of radical thinking, of thinking focused on the end and what is beyond the end, a decline of every Weltanschauung.

Marked by blackmail with misery and values, there is an intrusion of thinking oriented to means, a thinking that favors instrumental strategies over disastrous strategies. Together with mundane and operational eclecticism, crisis promotes all nostalgic and sentimental remakes from those of love to those of human rights, from those of fashion revivals to socialism in politics, and discourages everything regarded as adventurous. In this sense the wind has changed, and perspectives have survived only in the intention behind this intellectual blackmail with crisis. There is no crisis. We are living in a brilliant epoch; no one knows what might happen. That is our chance, which at the same time is our chance to pick up on radical pessimism again, the basis of which is the fact that everything is continually improving, and on the hidden charm of provocative analysis. In dealing with the epidemic of visibility menacing our entire culture today, we must, as Nietzsche quite correctly said, cultivate mendacious and deceptive clear-sightedness.

II. CONCEPTS OF THE END OF THE WORLD

Christoph Wulf

The Temporality of World-Views and Self-Images

World-view and self-image are indissolubly intertwined
with each other. The way man sees the world is the way
he sees himself; the way he conceives himself is the way
he conceives the world. Alterations in his view of the
world lead to alterations in his view of himself and vice
versa.

Time is the medium that binds a man's view of the
world with his view of himself. It follows, then, that alterations in man's view of the world and of himself are to an
essential degree alterations in his perception of time. The
dimensions of time connected with the world at large
differ from those connected with the individual. Our
concern is to establish the difference between these two.

The world, it is true, has not yet been destroyed, but
from the beginning mankind has seen the end of many
worlds. With the death of each and every human being a
specific world ceases to exist. Views and conceptions of
the world come and go with the emergence and disappearance of the generations of man. Owing to the reduc-
tionistic nature of the way mankind views and has viewed
the world, it is necessary, today more than ever before, to

put such mental attitudes behind us. The end of mankind's views of the world and the end of the world itself point one to the other. It is imperative to try and comprehend the world from the point of view of its end, doing so, however, before the eschatological catastrophe takes place.

The German word "Welt" (= world) has become an abstract temporal noun. It can be translated as the "life-bearing circle of the human community" and refers to the times and spaces of human existence. There is no evidence of this meaning in the pre-Christian era; it serves, in fact, as a translation of the Latin word "saeculum". In the 10th and 11th centuries, it appears in the meaning of "epoch", "era" analogous to "aion", and in the meaning of "generation". Only gradually did the word "world" become the equivalent of "mundus" and "kósmos". World retains the meaning of "circle of the earth's inhabitants", "existence in this world", and refers to a "self-contained whole, to universal fullness of any kind whatsoever". The word "world" is also used to designate "an in itself self-contained domain of this or that kind which, in its independence and autonomy, represents, as it were, a mini-universe", "the entirety of a spiritual sphere", or "the totality of the phenomena and facts that can be grasped by the mind and senses".

In summary, then, for our context, we have the following results of our etymological analysis:

1. "World" serves to designate a period of time; it implies the emergence and passing away of time; "world" is equivalent to "time".
2. "World" specifies the human commmunity; the place where one lives in contrast to uninhabited areas and the times before man existed.

3. "World" signifies a self-contained entity, a reduction of complexity to the limited unity of a world-view.

"World" is a heuristic concept which has arisen by an approach which involves exclusion and inclusion, destroys complexity and puts limits on candor. It implies the reduction of realities to signs which make it possible under pressure to comprehend things quickly, to make them as much as possible one's own in the shortest possible time.

From Husserl's concept of "Lebenswelt" (= living world, world of life), springs the reference to the way world and life are intertwined. Under the general concept of time, an encreasing gap has grown between the individual life-span and extended world-time. An ever-growing shortage of time, an acceleration of the conflict with the world, these are the results. How can a human being, within his restricted life-span, cope with the fact that the world is expanding beyond historic time and beyond the temporality of nature into a virtual infinity, with the discrepancy between the potentiality of an individual life and the general time limits of the world at large becoming intolerable? The increasing acceleration inherent in modern life makes it impossible to put an end to this growing discrepancy.

Adam and Eve's life in Paradise was outside time; they lived in a circumscribed world without knowledge of and the ability to judge between good and evil. Life in Paradise meant there was nothing external to it and nothing to come after is. Adam and Eve's world of perception was everything and was always available. Eating the apple from the Tree of Knowledge made a knowledge of evil unavoidable. Being driven out of Paradise brought privation and death into the life of man and, inevitably, evil followed. Now that life was finite, the balance was broken between life and the world; the world has become increasingly more comprehensive; a life-time does not suffice to gain contol over it.

Allowing for the possibility that during antiquity and the Middle Ages experience of life's shortness was not yet decisive, it is precisely this experience which has become, in modern times, the fundamental condition of life itself. It began with the decline of the old world: that Ptolemaic image of the world by which the earth was held to be the stationary centre round which sun and stars revolved, was replaced by the Copernican heliocentric view. Although centuries have passed since scientists started to act on this alteration of the world perspective, the view of the world that most people have rooted in their everyday consciousness is still Ptolemaic rather than Copernican. The changes have simply been too decisive for the everyday consciousness to comprehend their effects on the self-image. Dimensions of time that had, until then, been barely imaginable, suddenly began to reveal themselves: light years; celestial bodies whose light we can still see but which have probably long been extinguished. The dimensions of time that we can still imagine have been rendered null and void. Time's new dimensions have thrust individual lives with their limited time-spans into meaninglessness. On the one hand, a cosmos extended to incomprehensible limits with its corresponding time dimensions; on the other, a life stretching over a mere seventy to eighty years. With these cosmic time dimensions in view, the cyclic variation of the seasons, so rooted in man's everyday consciousness from antiquity, through the Middle Ages right up to modern times, and which become a yardstick for the aging process in man, has now lost its significance. The loss of the world as a place that man

could call his home seems unavoidable. The dimensions
of time as we knew them have suddenly been smashed
and the expanse of ether has become visible. Subsequently, mankind's need for time has become
boundless.

During their life times, the astronomists Copernicus,
Keppler and Rheticus were already aware of this shortage
of time. In order to be in a position to obtain precise
details about the alterations in the stars, time spans have
to be taken into consideration which far excede the life-
span of an individual. There was an inevitable correlation
between Descartes' attempt to develop a universal scientific methodology and the growing shortage of time.
Descartes' methodology lays claim to validity irrespective
of the individual human being and his life-span. The time
dimensions of the world and those of the individual
human being have once and for all been separated from
each other. The inability of the human being as the
"subject of history" to comprehend the world is a painful
thing. Even the generic subject "man" does not dispose
over the necessary time to do so. This is the reason why
progress has become such an obsession in modern life.
The shortage of time is now to be made good with pro-
gress-accelerated progress. The faster the human race
moves ahead, the sooner does it hope to be in a position
to cope with the immense demand for time. Similar
demands are made of the individual. Growth is the
watchword. It is, even in individual life, the only way to
cope with the finiteness of life and the limited time
available for learning as much about the world as possible.

The radical rupture between individual and cosmic
time dimensions has lead to the breaking down of the
binding force of meaning – whether for individual lives,

for epochs, or for the human species as a whole. Can meaning still be arrived at by science through knowledge? The time required for such has also been continually growing. Truth has become a product of time. Authority and consensus have been receding from view − at any rate since the beginning of the modern era. Scientists are finding it increasingly necessary to expand the boundaries of time. They have been trying, with growing ruthlessness, to satisfy their needs in this respect. The time still available to individual human beings is sacrificed to these demands. If we know more about the world today than has been known in any previous epoch, it still does not mean that the individual also knows more. Bacon was yet able to hope that, with the increase in knowledge, people could be made happy and paradise won back. For us today this hope has long been superceded by the conviction that an increase in knowledge is by no means a guarantee of happiness.

With their claim to universality, modern scientists have enforced the homogenization of individual life. Their aim is a knowledge gained over generations and guaranteed in its claim to validity. To achieve this, it is necessary to demand asceticism and a renunciation of the richness of life. The result justifies the renunciation of individual accomplishment. Nothing else is possible when knowledge has to be gained irrespective of the limits set by a man's life-span, using methods independent of the context. The individual life-span which thus results is, in an admittedly limited sense, the antithesis of cosmic infinity. By the end of the 18th century, the subject of cognition/knowledge was replaced by the ideal of causal laws. Their validity guaranteed that the individual lost his central place in the world of knowledge.

Almost as great are the difficulties to which our subject's constitution has been subject by history. In this respect, human identity has been called into question by the fact that the past can no longer be readily comprehended as being the past of the human race itself. The evolution of life provides the first indication of this. Where does the history of man begin? Where does it end? It undoubtedly begins long before the period of recorded history. But where is the borderline to the non-human? Is the history of the origins of life on earth already a part of the history of man? Here, too, the new dimensions of time have thrown wide open the views man has of the world and of himself. The pre-historic development of life on earth took up such an enormous amount of time. The consequence is that history, previously rooted in the concept of an assumed succession of generations, has now been transferred to the history of nature. The history of man is swallowed up by the history of life and of nature. In this regard, too, man experiences that sense of being lost in time. As a result, the significance of man for the world diminishes far more as the significance of the world for man. The views man has of himself and of the world are the product of an irreversible process altering man's whole conception of the dimensions of time. They are the product of a rational judgement which itself is the outcome of a process that has turned upside down the time dimensions of human life. Man cannot comprehend infinity; he does not even possess the power to grasp the enormous time dimensions of the finite world. By separating history from human nature, historical time becomes a dimension between a human being's lifetime and world time, particularly as a result of the dissociation of world and human history.

It is extremely difficult to avoid seeing human history as a history of progress, although a certain view of history has repeatedly arisen according to which the "Golden Age" is to be found at the beginning of the history of man, the periods after this being considered, rather, as periods of decline. Mostly, however, the history of man was seen as analogous to the development of the individual, a development which passed through various phases, the one built up on the other: childhood, adolescence, adulthood and old age. Correspondingly, historical development was usually conceived as the history of the expansion of mankind's reasoning powers. Only rarely were such considerations based on the belief that errors and foulty developments were also an inevitable part of the historical process. In most cases, though, the history of mankind has emerged as the story of the "life and sufferings of man", albeit it secular in form. We, today, are increasingly experiencing the indifference of time towards the reasoning powers of both the individual and the whole of mankind.

The "Age of Enlightenment" suffered from the realization that is was a late − possibly even too late − stage in human development. "Nous sommes venus tard en tout. Je l'ai dit et le redis. Regagnons le temps perdu" (Voltaire). Acceleration seemed the way out. Hence the present became the point of reference for all things, for all possibilities of human development. The concept of time, which for so long had been the medium for phenomena, itself became a power from which man expected something. On the other hand, time is indifferent to the things of the world; on the other, it is, in the life of human beings, the medium which has thrust itself upon their consciousness bei reason of its very scarcity. In the second half of the 18th century, as a result of Rainer Koselleck investigations, a new conception of time arose for modern times: "Time continues to be not only the form within which all historical happenings take place, but itself has taken on a historical quality. History, then, no longer takes place within the framework of time, for time has become a dynamic power in history itself." For man this means: it is responsible for the speed with which history now moves forward, but not for history itself. For Ernst Benz, this speed was the most important element in the secularization, and to which he attached more significance than to the replacement of belief in the end of the world by the concept of world improvement.

The measuring of time calls for a difference between movements and a range of difference that is accessible to our sense of perception. From this Kant concluded: Determination of the dimensions of time is not possible without the perception of a world outside the world of our inner consciousness; in other words, an inner sense of time is impossible without an outer sense of the same. An awareness of time establishes itself "from the need of our consciousness to be itself and remain so, although it is always forced to allow to be given something else − as its possibility to objects". Time is, to an extremely high degree, a part of man; simultaneously, though, it is something that is least of all available to us.

Nietzsche expressed it more clearly than anyone else: The unity of the subject as it reveals itself in the images the subject has of himself, is a product of the individual's limited life-span which does not allow him enough time to develop differing identities. The shortness of a life-span protects man from having his identity splitting up. Assuming that a very much longer life-span were possible, the development of various identities would be unavoidable. The result would be self-images at variance with one another.

Even in respect of man's internal organization, it will

be found that time is the decisive medium. The meaning of a subject's life forms itself within this dimension. As the generations succeed one another, so do the phases of life each with their specific socio-biological conditions. In both cases, the divisions are quite arbitrary and their meaning is, perhaps, to be found soonest in the attempt to impose a system of meaning and order upon that "flow of time" which is so indifferent to the human species. A subject's self-image is dependent of his reflections about the length of his life-span and on his powers of recollection, through which life's experiences are seen in relation to one another. It is also, though, dependent on the time structure of the movements that are registered — of the changes in each and every Self; in other words, on the time structure of the sense of perception. The views an individual has of himself and of the world are conditioned by experiences which are determined by the length of time occupied by a particular perception. The perceptive faculty of our sense-organs is structured like a raster and comprises elements of a constant dimension. According to this, then, intuition can be described as man's ability to comprehend the world using the means placed at his disposal by his own organic nature. By utilizing this ability, man is able to comprehend the world as objectified through nature.

Just as spatial measuring units are derived from the human body, so temporal ones are derived from the human life-span. However, it is the time shortage to which the human organism is subject that remains decisive. It is this that pushes man into avoiding an explanation of things as they are. Arriving at a clear explanation of any of the world's phenomena takes up a considerable amount of time; the time limitations so characteristic of modern life force one, therefore, to make use of symbols which can be abstracted from the things under examination and made readily available. As soon as it is no longer necessary to do everything oneself and to have everything as itself, we have two of the most important gains to be made by man in his search for an explanation of his own finiteness. It is not possible, of course, for a human being to keep himself shut up within the world of signs, symbols and technical terms; he must make use once more of his power of perception, otherwise he will sacrifice the increase in possibilities due to him as a result of the time gained.

When referring back from the dimensions of the world to the temporal dimensions of life and body, a decisive quantity is the *moment* which corresponds to the pulse rate and behind which our sense of perception can conceal so much. The body's smallest unit of time is, however, *sensation*, in other words the amount of time that elapses before a perception becomes a sensation, or the amount of time which we require to become aware of an impression made on our senses.

Our perception of the world and ourselves is bound up with the time dimensions of our body. If our life-span were a thousand times longer, we would experience differently from now. If we lifed only one thousandth of our life-span, we would again experience differently. Our knowledge and our capacity to gain knowledge cannot escape this fundamental relationship with time. The inner consciousness of time can only become a clear basis for the concept of time if the smallest unit of time arising from the function of the sense-organ is not, at the same time, that of the consciousness. This means that time consciousness overlaps the smallest individual unit of time. There is, in subjective experience, no equivalent to objectively identifiable synchronism. For if man did not exist, all stimulations would take place "simultaneously and separately" without there being an "earlier" or "later", without the happenings taking a chronological turn. It is the *moment* that first imposes a chronological sequence and order upon the stimulations operating on an organism, and, in turn, through the sub-noticeable joining together of successive units of this smallest time-span, time originates.

In the *moment*, the world stands still. A series of moments in which, respectively, time stands still, leads to the emergence of time consciousness. Time consciousness would then be something like a compromise to avoid the two extremes: a world standstill or world disintegration. In the moment, a fusion and concentration are taking place; within this there is more than one sensation; many sensations are concentrated within one moment. Jakob von Uexküll gives the following illustration of this: "The sequence of perception worlds, which proceeds chronologically, can be graphically represented as a perception world tunnel if each individual perception world is conceived two-dimensionally and then placed one after the other like discs. The thickness of each disc corresponds to a moment." Man's life-span does not then correspond to the row of discs, but to the threedimensional tunnel, his life-time, which consists of two-dimensional self-contained perception world discs.

If these considerations are taken further, the following conclusions can be drawn: an act of coherent consciousness is formed regardless of the fact that the individual parts are not synchronized. In their writings on psychology, William Stern and William James have dealt with this act of coherent consciousness under the concept of presence time which can last from one moment to several seconds. It is its content, though, that is decisive for its establishment as an act of consciousness.

Each state of consciousness is governed by time, and, indeed, in two senses of the word. For one, each state of consciousness creates its own time; secondly, it is contained within a certain time bound up with a subject's life-span which, in turn, ist bound up with world time through which it is determined. Consequently, the subject's views of the world and of himself possess a double reference to the time-conditioned state of consciousness. They are the result of a temporal process and produce a certain view of time. They are not without a connection to time. Simultaneously, though, they are also destroyed by the course of time. There is no self-image, no world-view that can outlast the course of time. Only by the power of recollection can they remain in a subject's mind; only through man's use of this faculty are they kept alive. The faculty of memory has become the very centre of the conflict between an individual's time dimensions and those of the world.

Man's views of the world and of himself can be seen as part of an attempt, if not to close the gap between the time dimensions of the individual and those of the world, at least to make it bearable. They establish a meaning to life, make the subject feel at home in the world, and help conceal from him the brutality of this temporal difference. They induce him to delude himself about the hopelessness of his ephemeral existence by presenting themselves as certainties. If, however, science and philosophy have come to one realization, it is that these views man has of himself and of the world are, by their very nature, temporary, false and illusory, and that their dependence on time cannot be considered radically enough. For it is in this dependence that the reasons for their transitory character are to be found. The views man has of the world are anthropomorphous and, by throwing light on something else, become different. These world-views are, in the last analysis, the views man has of himself, his self-image, for in this world he only ever meets himself without really grasping the fact. Correspondingly, man's views of himself are also only reflections of the world-views. As long as they remain valid, there is no escape from this reciprocal shifting of world-view and self-image. In order, therefore, to achieve a radical clarification of the situation, it will be necessary to challenge their validity. Not until the validity of world-views and self-images is effectively challenged will new perspectives begin to arise.

The difference between the individual's life-span and the world's temporal dimensions has become so unbearable for the subject that he feels the simultaneous end of his own existence and that of the world, as predicted in mankind's apocalyptic and eschatological phantasms, to be an alleviation of individual destiny. If a man must perish, the disappearance of the human species reconciles him with his destiny. Today, for the first time, men have the possibility to bring about the end of the world simultaneously with their own end. These phantasms exercise a peculiar fascination. Possibly, they are bringing to light archaic urges of an immolatory or self-sacrificial nature. It is a temptation about which we do not know whether one day or other mankind will succumb to it. Such sacrificial urges have appeared again and again in the manic phantasms of such dictators as Hitler. Be that as it may: the possibility that today man himself, if given a chance, can bring the world to an end, has led to new perspectives for a re-evaluation of the history of mankind of which we are only now beginning to gain an idea. One of these is the necessity to break down world, world-views and self-images by demonstrating the time element in them, and to replace them with the candor of astonishment and radical questioning.

—————————————————————

Translation by Robert Golding

Dieter Lenzen

Disappearing Adulthood

Childhood as Redemption

0. The transition from total to partial apocalypses, i. e.
the inclination to see global downfall even in the threat
posed to one individual element of our culture, is one
aspect following in the train of enlightenment. To quote
one example from the turn of the last century, disastrous
consequences were attributed to the decline of education
and upbringing as the status symbols of a particular social
stratum in connection with the decline of the Wilhelm-
enian Empire in Germany. The latest partial apocalypses
include Neil Postman's vision, which received an avid
reception at least in Germany, of "Disappearing Childhood" (1983), the basic thesis of which will, by the way, be
found preformulated in the works of Karl Kraus: if it was
the invention of the rotary printing press which, for Kraus,
predicated the approach of the "last days of mankind",
then it was the spread of the visual media which, as we
know, provoked Postman to claim that childhood was in
the process of disappearing. As television, in his view,
finally revealed all secrets to children, from those of

sexuality to those of war — the very secrets of which the adult world was composed — there was, according to Postman, a danger of children becoming indistinguishable from adults. The child as a sociological type, he stated, was dying out.

This kind of news is well calculated to spread alarm and despondency among people of every political conviction. But the fact that this piece of news is able to provoke dismay shows that it is false. The concern regarding the continuation of childhood that can be thus provoked is only conceivable if children as a type enjoy such a broad degree of estimation that their disappearance can be understood as something undesirable. Neil Postman's book is thus, in itself, the most convincing proof that a statement diametrically opposed to his thesis is, in fact, true: it is not childhood that is disappearing, but the status of the adult — brought about by an expansion of childlike aspects in all spheres of our culture.

As I would like to devote my attention today to a problem that reaches beyond this thesis, the question, namely, of the relationship between the expansion of childhood and a simultaneous accumulation of apocalyptic anxieties, at least in Germany, I shall content myself with a short sketch by way of justification for my thesis, especially as I have already put this thesis forward in book form.

1.1. If we first consider the plane of phenomena we will notice a lively tendency to extend childhood, to expand it into all phases of life. This is apparent from the successive extensions of the time young people spend at educational establishments or in training which, in Germany, already amounts to 25 years for about one third of the young people born in any given year. It can also be seen in the gradual incapacitation of adult citizens by the benefits bestowed by the Welfare State.

From unemployment benefit and educational grants to public assistance, the German state each year provides welfare payments that already exceed, in number, the country's population figure. This means that there are already a by no means small number of German citizens who eke out a living not from one but from several public sources with the result that they are no longer responsible for themselves: the State, not for nothing personified as a father figure in many languages, has taken over this responsibility for them.

If one then considers the explosion of pedagogical professions, the members of which not only accompany one through one's pre-school and school life but will still be found in clubs, hospitals, at holiday resorts, at one's place of work, in old people's homes and, last but not least, beside one's deathbed to ease the transition from this life to the next, it is clear that this type of pedagogical care at all stages of life must, of necessity, turn adults into children even on the surface.

1.2. These *superficial phenomena* are accompanied by a *structural* feature. For if one compares the typical life of an individual still living in the traditional society of the nineteenth century with that of a young person of our day and age, a far-reaching change will become evident: the traditional course of life was organized cyclically. It consisted of a sequence of life-phases that was more or less obligatory for all, beginning with that of the as-yet unbaptised new-born child, via puberty, adolescence, to matrimony, parenthood etc., to name only a few. The transition from one phase of life to the next was governed by rites in which the community performed physical and psychical operations on the person to be initiated (baptism, circumcision, wedding ceremony, ritual confinement etc.).

The function of these rites, in the course of which the person to be initiated was removed from his accustomed surroundings, sometimes to the accompaniment of dramatic circumstances, and subjected to painful procedures and instruction, was to extinguish the individual of the preceding life-phase and to permit him to be born again as the "new man" of the next stage. This pattern of death and rebirth was repeated several times in each lifetime and had a dual effect: the individual was, so to speak, practising dying (and, in dying, living again) and he experienced himself as a person getting older and having to come to terms with the fact of death.

If we contrast this with the life sequence of a contemporary, we will see that most transitional rites have disappeared, that those which remain have degenerated into mere family festivals (baptisms, weddings and funerals) that have lost their original functions, and that, at the same time, people's attempts to initiate *themselves* on their own responsibility are unsuccessful.

This latter statement can be illustrated with the help of the example of the pregnancy test. Whereas in earlier times the rite of "annunciation" by priests or at least doctors fulfilled the function of the transition from the state of womanhood to that of coming motherhood, the pregnancy test kit from the pharmacy leaves a woman to her own devices with the result that she only becomes physically, not mentally pregnant. A transition can only succeed if delegates from society such as shamans and priests *declare* the person concerned to have died and been born again in a new phase of life, as is clearly seen in the still widespread church rite of marriage. A couple cannot declare itself to be a married couple.

The fact that the transitional rites which formerly marked the move from one phase of life to the next have now
disappeared means that people in today's cultures never
proceed beyond the first phase, that of the child. This is
the *structural* expansion of childhood in our culture.

1.3. In addition to the *phenomena* of the expansion of
childhood in our everyday lives and the *structures* of the
conservation of childhood caused by the absence of transitions in the course of life, we should also consider a
third, *mythological* element that allows us to point out a
first connection between the status of childhood and the
acceleration of the apocalyptic element in our culture.
For it can be demonstrated that the expansion of childhood or, rather, the disappearance of adulthood is
accompanied by a deification of childhood which, though
not without precedent, is, however, unparalleled in its
extent. To a previously unknown extent, our everyday
culture is permeated with symbols attributing god-like
characteristics to children. Whether it be pop singers
wishing that they were "young again", or a guide to
successful child photography disclosing tricks on how to
get the kiddies to laugh when the camera is on them, or
right-wing conservative groups threatening the population
with trouble "unless they become as children" (i. e.
capable of manipulation), or trashy Nazi picture-books
equating children with "wealth", or anti-atomic-energy
demonstrators who take their children along and drape
their "innocent" bodies with anti-atomic-energy slogans
– the appeal is always to the old myth, the myth of the
divinity, the sacredness of children brought about by their
purity. On the occasion of the colloquium on "the sacred"
held in Berlin in 1984, I explained the mechanism whereby attributes of godliness such as the (childlike) laughter

mentioned in Zoroaster or in Vergil's fourth eclogue were assigned to earthly children in order to sanctify them, and, through them, to sanctify themselves as adults, so I shall not go into the matter any further here. It is, however, important to remember that it was not just *any* attributes of divinity that were bestowed on these thoroughly normal children but, in particular, those attributes which belonged to those deities who appear in mythology as saviour figures. In addition to Christ these include Apollo, Dionysos, Heracles and Mithras. They share, for example, the distinction of having come into this world "per natum ex virgine" (by virgin birth). Is it too far-fetched to wonder whether the rapidly spreading techniques of genetic reproduction, which produce the "unnatural" propagation and birth of children, do not also lead to the deification of these fruits of medical activities? Finally, something that was otherwise reserved for the gods but which caught and held the imagination of men as a phantasm for centuries has actually become feasible.

2. The Jewish-Christian tradition made a particular contribution to this piece of wishful thinking. The pious misinterpretation of the pericope in Matthew 18, verses 1 to 6, according to which we all have to become as children, has a long history. Nietzsche sharply criticised this image in his "Antichrist": ". . .; the kingdom of heaven belongs to *children*. This is no new belligerent creed that raises its voice – it is already there, it was there from the beginning: it is a spiritual return to childishness. Physiologists at least are familiar with cases of infantile regression, due to functional atrophy or to delayed puberty . . .".

The institutionalisation of this message was taken over by educational science from theology in the 19th century. Many educationalists have proclaimed it. Maria Montes-

sori, the famous educational reformer, stated with un-
mistakable clarity and closely following Emerson: "The
child is the eternal Messiah, continually descending
among fallen men to lead them into the Kingdom of
Heaven" (Montessori). The extent to which this educational gospel also included rendering the mother holy, is
shown by a quotation from Ellen Key, the author of the
epoch-making book "The Century of the Child" written at
the turn of the last century: "The time will come in which
the child will be looked upon as holy, even when the
parents themselves have approached the mystery of life
with profane feelings; a time in which all motherhood will
be looked upon as holy, if it is caused by a deep emotion
of love, and if it has called forth deep feelings of duty"
(Key).

This was the educational resumption of one of the
popular motifs of the Romantic Movement: holy child
and holy mother, to be found in numerous works, from
Schlegel's "Lucinde" to Novalis' "Heinrich von Ofter-
dingen".

Just as this "feminist" trail of the deification of mother
and child could be traced back to the High Middle Ages
and the early days of the veneration of the Virgin Mary, a
second element of this deification process is closely related to the history of the Christian church. If the reforma-
tion was followed by a pitiless persecution of the Ana-
baptists, whose hope for salvation rested in adults, not in
infants, then this is yet another brick in the wall of the
flight from adulthood which had arisen with the dogma of
original sin and the baptism of infants, and which had,
even after the Age of Enlightenment, recurred in absolutely secular forms, last but not least in psychoanalysis,
where the path to salvation ends in a regression. Those
who wish to treat their neuroses by maturing under anal-

ysis have to return to the stations of their childhoods: ". . . unless you be converted, and become as little children, you shall not enter into the kingdom of heaven".

What Gottsched had warned us about in his translation of Fontenelle, that the world might "become completely barbaric once more", i. e. that it might "decay into childhood" (Fontenelle) has been explained time and again and with increasing frequency over the past 150 years as the royal road to salvation. This recipe for redemption via a collective return to childhood, via a flight from adulthood, via a deification of the children seems paradoxical and would appear to be an expression of the most recent confusion of all categories, of the differentiation between adults and children. We must, therefore, ask what function this collective paradox of our day and age may have.

3. In my opinion the already-mentioned characteristic of this simple belief in redemption via a totalisation of childhood would seem to be the expression of a mechanism with the help of which a culture is attempting to regenerate itself. In his "Politikos" Plato has described cataclysms with the help of which a regeneration of culture takes place, i. e. that a regression from adults to children could cause people to disappear completely in the end, opening up the way to a renewal of the world. We can see from this that the phenomenon of expanding childhood observable on all sides can be interpreted as an apocalyptic process. Correspondingly, the disappearance of adults could be understood as the beginning of a cosmic regeneration process based on the destruction of history.

Mircea Eliade has shown that a culture may possess a need to destroy history because the consciousness of historicity is probably difficult for the individual to bear. It reminds him of the finite nature of the individual and produces insecurity in view of the high relativity of the fate of the individual by comparison with the history of the species. Primitive cultures, in Eliade's opinion, thus often live in the consciousness of an eternal present, or they celebrate regeneration cults to destroy history as the story of their tribes.

Eschatological conceptions of history such as that held by the Jews no longer deny the existence of their history; it is made bearable by the hope that, one day, it will cease because an eschatological tendency is predicated for it. If we consider the progress-oriented theory of history held by modern Europeans in the light of the continuation of this tradition, we can, as Eliade does, interpret this as a medium for the satisfaction of those who may not believe in a destruction of history along eschatological lines but who have, nevertheless, to cope mentally with insight into historicity. For them, history becomes a consolation as an object made by man and aimed at improving life.

As far as the valuation of the observed explosion of childhood and the simultaneous disappearance of adults is concerned, it becomes plain that this process is incompatible with a modern conception of history. This is clearly a non-modern regeneration phenomenon where the question that poses itself is whether it should be attributed to the pattern of the periodic destruction of history or to that of eschatology.

4. If one recalls the precise structure of Jewish-Christian eschatology, it soon becomes clear that the erosion of the childlike is rooted in the doctrine of redemption. In the epistles of Paul to the Corinthians (2 Corinthians Chapter 8, Verse 9), to the Romans (Chapter

8, Verse 3), and to the Galatians (Chapter 4, Verse 4 ff.) the key message supporting this interpretation becomes abundantly clear: The pre-existent Son of God, a child, that is, became what we are, namely people, adult people; as one such adult He was killed in order that we might become what He is: children of God.

This means that reducing culture to childlike innocence and deifying children within it holds out the prospect of the redemption of all those promises made in the gospels: the "summum bonum", happiness, "imitatio dei", in short, all that Paul offered: light, truth and life. And it means delivery from the sins which we committed and still commit as adults, delivery from the death that is our lot, from "malum".

5. What do contemporaries consider this "malum" to be? What is so depressing about it that a culture is ready to throw in the towel before the end of history, before doomsday, the Day of Judgement "in illo tempore"?

Two fundamentally different possibilities are conceivable to interpret this process. On the one hand the redemption wish expressed in the expansion of childhood could be understood as a substitute for the Day of Judgement in the sense that we have lost belief that that day will come and are ourselves forced to take action — the substitute action of regression. On the other hand the phenomenon could also be seen as a preparation for the real End of the World in which the signs for the coming destruction of history are veritably engendered. As we have already seen in Plato's writings, the tendency to revert to childhood is one such sign. It indicates the path to the disappearance of the individual which must, at some future time, be followed by the creation of the new individual.

The statement made by someone who was demonstrating with his children against nuclear power and which was quoted in Germany's largest weekly newspaper "DIE ZEIT" recently fits in well with this interpretation:

"Life should run in the opposite direction: we should come into the world as old people, get progressively younger and finally end up as children" (Ginsburg).

It is impossible to say that one or the other interpretation is definitively correct. However much they differ from one another — the simulation of doomsday on the one hand and the preparation for it on the other — they still resemble each other. One feature which they share is obviously a veritably libidinous relationship to the apocalypse.

6. Why, one might ask, is this apocalyptic urge enjoying such a vogue "in illud tempus" — in these years — "in hoc tempore"? As this question has been the subject of numerous considerations recently, I only intend to pursue the answer to the extent that the demonstrable phenomenon of the expansion of childhood offers help where other approaches fail.

Kant provided one answer. In "The End of All Things" he wrote: "But why do people expect an end of the world at all? . . . The reason . . . seems to be that their reason (in the sense of "Vernunft") tells them that the continuation of the world is only of value if the reasonable beings in it correspond to the final purpose of their existence, but that if this is not to be achieved, creation itself seems to be pointless to them . . ." (Kant).

From this it follows that the periodic appearance of apocalyptic moods might have its foundation, among other things, in the fact that, as the life of the individual only makes sense if it is threatened, if life today is suffering from a loss of meaning, that can only be combatted by producing a mood of catastrophe.

If we consider J. Derrida's analysis in this context we come across an answer which, to some extent, could only be derived from its extension. Lord Byron had provided the motif in his "Don Juan", finished in 1824, that the end of the world was, in fact, no longer nigh − it had actually long begun in the form of an internal death caused by coldness. If our day and age, as Derrida thinks, can thus be considered postapocalyptic because the apocalypse − even the atomic one − has already taken place in thousandfold form in the media, and because there is no veritable apocalypse left to come, especially as there would be no audience for it anyway, then these findings do not yet provide an answer to the question concerning the reasons for this desire for apocalypse. Far from any causal determination it can, nevertheless, be said that an implication − if not an actual sense − of *this* kind of "apocalypsia" (to treat it as a disease) lies in the prevention of a real end of the world. Or, to put it bluntly: nobody is really frightened that the world is coming to an end, but a life without anxiety is much too dangerous.

7. If one compares the two explanations for the recent outbreak of "apocalypsia" − making sense of the situation by threatening an apocalypse and preventing the end of the world by symbolically simulating it − then the phenomenon of disappearing adulthood acquires particular significance in its combination with the simultaneous deification of children.

As this double phenomenon corresponds to a bringing forward of redemption to this side of the End of All Things, the sense-making role of this fear of the end of the world disappears for the people in our culture; life loses its sense insofar as this sense, as Kant said, is produced by the threat to it. This is matched, on the individual plane, by the renunciation of the rites of transition from one phase of life to the next, because remaining in the childhood phase, as we have seen, means that there is no learning how to die: the fact of death is thus ignored. But if, via the disappearance of the adult estate and the deification of the children, i. e. via redemption in one's own lifetime, an anxiety deficit arises, and if not to be frightened is far too dangerous, then collective consciousness has to create sources which will serve as replacements for the fear of death which was traditionally implanted by the cyclical course of life. There is a lot of evidence for the argument that the present boom in fears of global destruction processes such as the fear of AIDS, of war or the death of our forests fulfil this replacement function. The presentation of this threat in the media, however, can play a decisive role as a possible genuine threat. For firstly the fear of a real end of the world on a global scale is public mischief. Anyone who insists that this might happen has no idea of biochemistry, that is, of the power of organic matter to regenerate itself; and when he talks of an apocalypse he is referring rather to his own chances of survival than to those of the universe.

Secondly, an occurrence such as the accident of Chernobyl and its political consequences show that people may be prepared to do anything apart from allowing their fears of what may befall to be removed. Regional elections which took place in the Federal Republic of Germany shortly after the Soviet reactor failure resulted in a considerable loss of votes for the very party which is almost synonymous with the call for a renunciation of atomic energy: the "Greens". For if this party came to power and were able to put its program into practice, decreeing the closing-down of atomic power stations, this would remove a quite considerable source of anxiety for which no replacement is in sight.

I should thus like to assume that something rather like a delicately adjusted balance exists, an equilibrium between the dismantling of expectations of salvation in the Hereafter or their transference to the Here and Now on the one hand, and the building up of simulatively generated fears as replacements on the other, so that Kant and Derrida both mutually come into their own to a certain extent.

Not, of course, in the sense that the simulation of destruction demonstrated by Derrida is the precondition for the obsolescence of a real end of the world, but in the sense that these simulations are (also) a consequence, indeed a stabilizing surrogate for the anxiety deficits which result from the self-fulfilment of the expectation of salvation in a life standardized to the requirements of childlikeness.

8. This connection can be explained even more clearly if we make use of considerations which Hans Blumenberg put forward in his study on the relationship between life-time and world-time. The eschatological expectation of the Jewish-Christian tradition, explains Blumenberg, had, in addition to the meaning-engendering function describ-ed by Kant, yet another function: to pass on the consola-tion that it would one day be possible to re-establish the identity of life-time and world-time, still present in para-dise, in a negative way by the fact that world-time would come to an end in the same way as life-time. This idea nourished the belief held not only by the early Christian churches – and by people around the turn of the last millenium – that they were God's elect, but also held by

paranoiacs such as Adolf Hitler. They basked in the hope
that their lives would end with the end of the world,
whether in the normal course of events or by their own
doing.

Nothing more than such a synchronisation of life-time
with world-time underlies the thinking of the Enlightenment in which the redemption initiated by God is replaced by the independent activities of human beings aimed at
guiding progress to the culmination of the "good life" —
that life which, logically, can only be understood as the
perpetuation of this world here below. Against this background the necessity for a mutual connection between the
disappearance of adulthood and the spread of fears
regarding the end of the world should be spotlighted once
more:

Both phenomena serve one and the same purpose,
namely the synchronisation of life-time and world-time,
and both phenomena work towards one another to a
certain extent. The expansion of childhood conveys the
tendency to extend life-time, the fear of the End offers
the opportunity of shortening world-time. At the intersec-
tion of the trends characterized by these two contrary
graphs lies the hope that one might have the best of both
worlds: first, everlasting, childlike life "in hoc tempore"
and, second, a nasty End of the World, the contemplation
of which might be well adapted to dissipate the boredom
resulting, of necessity, from the first.

Translation by Philip N. Hewitt

III. BEYOND APOCALYPSE

Edgar Morin

Approaches to Nothingness

Among the numerous ways of approaching the phenomenon of Nothingness is to stress the anthropological dimension, which relates to an archaic or primordial Nothingness: that Nothingness which is linked to the awareness of death. At issue is not an awareness of death in terms of the ability to sense mortal danger, a faculty possessed by probably every living creature. What is meant is an awareness that is directly connected with the development of human language. Just like human language, our awareness is linked to an awareness of death. In this sense, death is by no means to be understood only as material annihilation since all the matter of every organism is preserved, altered, and reutilized in the chemical cycles of life − it is, in short, recycled back to nature. What is annihilated in death is only the individual as subject. This becomes clearer as soon as one explicitly examines the term "subject", which has absolutely no connection with the concepts of sensitivity or affectivity.

Rather, "subject" is the term for any individual who places himself at the center of a self-conceived world so as to observe and influence the rest of the universe from this action center, that is, to take it in from this center. As subject, the individual places himself at the center of his own world, self-centers himself as it were, whereby no valuation whatsoever is expressed. The result, in Hegel's terms, is that all behaviors and actions of the subject exist in the light of the "For itself".

Nevertheless, this subject is by no means active only for itself but rather also for an extended subjectivity, that is, for his family, his group, his society. In any case, being at the center of his own world means relating constantly only to oneself, even when the subject relates to something other than himself.

In connection with the question about the end of the world, about its annihilation, it thus remains to be noted that for every subject the end of *his* world is always the end of *the* world. In the history of human ideas of Nothingness as the end of the world, as the end of a subject's world, humans began early in attempting to avert their gaze from it by means of such things as myths and superstitions − both of which preached the continuation and return of life. In later ages in which individual fears intensified, myth and superstition were supplanted by the historical belief in the coming of salvation, in rebirth, and in the resurrection. This reorientation is found in the occidental world, that is, in those areas that adhered to Abrahamic religions − the Christian, Islamic, and Jewish faiths. Buddhism is a notable exception, for although the fundamental religious ideas remained unaffected, Buddhism inverts that relation and teaches a yearning for Nothingness, a keen desire to liberate oneself in this world from the suffering caused by the world. The only way to redemption as postulated by Buddhism is the detachment from the egocentrism of the self and from subjectivity.

Familiar from time immemorial, this problem of the gnawing work of death has become virulent in the modern, secularized societies, in which Nothingness resurfaces in another way. This change involves the following characteristic dialectic. Where a progressive annihilation — nihilism — is found in occidental societies, modern nihilists are turning to ostensibly long-abandoned ancient religions because these now appear to be the sole antidote to Nothingness. In France particularly, this contemporary, yet thoroughly classical, dialectic was demonstrated at an early time by Montaigne and Pascal. According to it, human beings believe not because they have inherited or adopted articles of faith from their fathers; nor do they believe for rational reasons. They adhere to their faith because they must free themselves from this manifest Nothingness, because they want to liberate themselves from it. Existential philosophy, which brought the Nothingness of death into the center of being itself, has attempted to reflect the penetration of this Nothingness into the thinking and life of our time.

But in addition to this possibility of coping with the permeation of Nothingness by turning to religion or philosophy, in addition to the possibility of discussing it primarily in connection with human existence, the world, and thinking, one should consider the very current and extremely brutal advances of Nothingness into the cosmos, into what is actually real, onto the earth as a planet, and into history. When speaking of the incursion of Nothingness, one must speak of very different kinds of incursion, which can be dealt with not only in chronological but also in mythological sequence. In the past twenty years, humans have completely changed their universe. They have even switched it. For about twenty years humans have recognized that the universe is strewn with different galaxies. The knowledge that a certain type of radiation is reaching us from three different directions in the universe has convinced us that this universe is based on a primordial detonation, a kind of explosion. It has since been necessary to abandon both the classical notion of a physics extended in space and time, that is, a spatio-temporal universe, and the notion of a mechanical, self-contained, and constantly self-regenerating universe. Science has made the conjecture plausible that the universe originated from an explosion. This perspective, however, assumes nothing other than that every form of materiality, every form of reality of the universe, was created from a void, from Nothingness.

Time no longer follows from time; space is no longer measured in temporal categories. Science's big-bang theory takes us back to an original Nothingness, to an initial explosion, a primeval detonation, with this Nothingness being attributed such intensity and such magnitude that it was helped spark the birth of things.

If this universe was born from a Nothingness, from a void, it is nevertheless not heading toward the Nothingness but rather "only" toward the annihilation of its construed or organized nature. In connection with the question about the density and quantity of matter, it is currently still quite disputable whether this universe is unalterably heading toward general vaporization or dissipation, eventually to leave only a huge amount of particles scattered in space, or whether, on the contrary, this general diffusion and scattering has already ended, that is, whether a devolution toward reconcentration is in process, with this universe perhaps again becoming dense enough to set off another explosion that could give rise to an altogether different recreation of something altogether different, although not the Eternal Recurrence evoked by

Nietzsche. In modern terms, the universe is conceived of as being caught up in that movement which — proceeding from the beginning as marked by the mystery of its birth, its emergence from Nothingness, to the end as marked by the problem of the universe's development — leads to annihilation, to Nothingness.

In addition to these two forms of the Nothingness, the proemial and the terminal, the primordial and the eschatologic, there remains a third form that is used in the effort to comprehend the advance of Nothingness. One could call it the autological form. Such a universe is based on no foundation, has no center, knows no genetic God, does not exist in all eternity. It is an acentric and polycentric universe, a world without aprioristic laws since our known laws of the universe develop with the world cotemporally and coextensively. Clearly, it is a world without a program, without divine Providence, without becoming. This world, which knows no foundation and no creator, which creates itself, engenders itself, generates itself, unfolds in the context of myriad autocreative and self-producing processes: the stars and atoms, of which there are billions.

Having been created from a primeval explosion, such a world is actually paradoxical in nature, for although it tends toward relatively slow, total annihilation, it takes shape through deformation, is integrated and organized in the context of disintegration. In purely quantitative terms, this world born of an explosion could be characterized as fluctuation approaching precisely what the mystics at one time wanted to refer to as mystery.

The universe is not born of the design or act of a genetic God, particularly since the genetic God in the Bible is only a degenerate God. The universe emerges from the process of the infinite retreating upon itself, as if this infinite were characterized by a kind of impurity. This retraction of the infinite upon itself results in a fall, a plunge; it resembles a fissure or crack in a glass vessel. Concepts like a fissure or crack are quite useful as metaphors and are just as appropriate as the closely related metaphor of the big bang. In any case, the movement leads to a countermovement, that is, to a universe that creates and produces itself. This universe is paradoxical in nature because in it there is in fact complexity, complexes, and autogenetic organizations that nevertheless followed from phenomena of destruction.

But this complex universe has still other paradoxes. There are moments in which the complexities or the complex parts give birth to themselves in the phenomena of scatter, of turbulent fermentation. In such a universe, the result is a reduction of Nothingness. This process was first observed in quantum physics, in microphysics, thanks to the work of Max Planck at the beginning of this century. According to his as yet unchallenged assertion, matter assumes the material form of a corpuscle or a wave. Simultaneously, the microphysical processes can be localized somewhere between the real and Nothingness. These processes are catalyzed between the real and the possible and in connection with their being observed by a researcher. Today, even the smallest or slightest form of organization within the nature of this universe is no longer referred to with that ghostly, though calculable, unit of measure known as the quark but rather with concepts like strings or superstrings. This metaphor permits the dissolution of the substantiality of what exists or what is being observed.

Beyond this there is a further reduction of the real. Our universe, subdivided into space and time, our world of the distinction and differentiation between things, objects, and phenomena is reduced to a different kind of reality. This other, new reality, which is becoming necessary above and beyond existing reality, has neither distinctions nor differentiations, neither definition nor space and time. It has already been the subject of great philosophic and scientific speculation and thought. The theories on this new reality teach that links and reciprocal influences of two microphysical objects are possible at a speed unimaginable to us, one that is infinitely great, probably far greater than that even of light. For us it is difficult to conceive of this speed, at which space and time are no longer separate; the indubitable discovery of the separation of space and time is decisive for our universe. For us it is considered certain that the light we perceive when gazing at the stars at night does not reach us at the moment it is radiated but that it has been on its way for millions of light years, reaching us at the moment it is perceived. We have long since lost the possibility of true universality. This space and this time, the distinction in which we imagine our universe to be rooted, no longer have a theoretical basis and can thus no longer be differentiated. This is where the axiom of ancient physics comes in according to which entities that have already had a link with each other, i. e., which have already interacted, essentially can no longer be separated and thus continue to interact. Even though differentiated within space and time, entities that have influenced each other in essence can no longer be differentiated. In this way the unreal has crept in and may have become the chief aspect of our reality. Reality gives birth to itself; it creates itself. Our reality is born at the same time as our organization. Because we, as organized beings, produce our own reality, we depend on organized things. We need the world to be organized because our reality follows from organization.

This self-organized reality develops at the seam, at the phenomenal fringe of things that theoretically defies formulation, that bears no name, and whose presence we surmise. At issue is thus a reduction of the real and the arrival of a different reality that we find difficult to name. For lack of a better term, we could call it "emptiness", with the term signifying the renunciation of any specific definition. This problem is a classic philosophical one to which Hegel tried to find a solution. He held that the absolute idea of being is identical with the idea of nothing, that is, of the absence of any limitation or definition. In this line of thought, antithetical ideas are simultaneously the same. Surely, the problem can be named, but we cannot call it "being" since that always embraces "nothing" as well, bringing us back to emptiness or to Nothingness again. Even the previously suggested term "chaos" must not be confounded with disorder but rather associated with indefiniteness, with the indefinite, which subsumes the possibility of disorder or order. Compared with the first two ways of thinking about Nothingness, this one can be called the ontological approach.

Another approach to Nothingness poses the question about the contemporary situation of the human being in the universe. This anthropic concept of Nothingness has already been addressed and discussed in astrophysics. It holds that every notional idea of the universe must from the very outset take into consideration that the universe is capable of producing life, thinking, and human beings. However, although this universe is able to create life and thinking, it remains extremely improbable that humans are the only living beings of this universe or even the only ones on the planet earth to possess consciousness and the ability to think. Drawn from the thinking of Teilhard de Chardin, this argument holds that the complexity, organization, life, and thinking in the universe are in the minority. Aside from the question of whether or not we are alone, there remain destruction, waste, disorder, all phenomena subsumed under the second law of thermodynamics — the price we must pay. The supposition that the universe is based on a kind of silent will or silent intention given to the increasing arrangement and augmentation of organizational development is an optimistic vision of the world in a tragic context.

Nevertheless, even less optimistic visions of this tragedy are known to exist, ones according to which the development of the human being, of thinking, and of consciousness represent an aberration within the general disaster of a basically or ultimately tragic universe. The question of whether life is a mishap is still undecided. Perhaps Martians do indeed exist; maybe we receive news from travelers from space but from other expanses, from time, perhaps from our future. Vice versa, there are thermodynamic arguments that life is neither mishap nor chance. In any case, though, the hope of being able to legitimate or penetrate the universe with human logic is systematically destroyed. Even the place and mission of the human race itself are no longer logically tenable. The assertion that the human is an absurd being in the midst of a rational world has become totally insufficient where contrary statements, too, can lay claim to validity: because the universe appears decodable to our rationality, it is becoming basically absurd for our rationality. In this line of reasoning, the universe is becoming absurd because human rationality is able to operate only with the aid of causality, of sense, and of purposefulness, but to our rationality it appears to have no causal roots, no sense, and no purpose.

In ancient times an Athenian philosopher posed the

question about the sphinx in the human being. He did not mean the problem of Oedipus, who presented the Sphinx his question, but rather raised the question of the "sphinxity" of humans themselves, the riddle that we carry within us and that we have assigned ourselves to solve. This problem is still unsolved and is continually posed anew. The advances we have made in understanding ourselves since ancient times have now reached a point at which thinking is supposed to reason out not only the human sphinx but the sphinx of the universe as well.

There is yet another, smaller Nothingness, one that is more regional in comparison with the universe: the Nothingness of the sun as a solar Nothingness. Although the sciences have by no means studied this form of Nothingness exhaustively yet, there seems to be no doubt that our sun is the successor of a long series of previous suns imploded or exploded one by one, suns that disintegrated into particles, and have long since ceased to exist. We are able to predict the vitality of our sun, calculating its remaining lifespan at ten billion years. We currently believe it to be mature and figure it to be four billion years old. Nevertheless, the sun is heading for its death. Long before the death of the sun, however, life on earth will have vanished, unless by then human beings have found other ways of emigrating to planets, other sun systems, more mature suns.

Another form of Nothingness is the thermonuclear, which, unlike the solar Nothingness, brings us back closer to our notion of the "end of the world". The thermonuclear weapon that humans have created is quite comparable to a small sun, though lacking its perfection since the weapon must first go through melting, fusion, or, better, splitting. We must not and cannot trust these weapons; we know too little about the potential explosive power they unleash and about the way to handle them. This thermonuclear threat is increasing quantitatively, for the more weapons there are, the more they spread to all points of the world and the more frequent the opportunities become to use them. To the extent that humans think in apocalyptic categories, cataclysms, and catastrophes relating to thermonuclear Nothingness, one can make out a topos of human history, particularly that of the Occident. In a certain way thermonuclear weapons are only a rebirth of occidental mythology — with a realistic argument added by virtue of the fact that these weapons are energetic-physical, i. e., really able to annihilate.

This flaming sword of the angel of destruction leads to another paradox. With the threat of its destructive potential, this flaming sword has paradoxically spared the human race from a world war since Hiroshima and Nagasaki and has kept local wars to their limited scale. The awareness among the population at large that the annihilation of the human race is quite possible is impressed even more clearly in the awareness of the political or military leaders of the great powers, which are prevented from going to war with each other by the very thermonuclear weapons they make.

Putting this paradox even more crassly, that is precisely why the human race depends on the intensive present and on the strong awareness of Nothingness, including thermonuclear Nothingness, in order to ward off and avoid this Nothingness.

Inferences can be drawn from this. The different forms of Nothingness pointed out here converge and flow together. The Nothingness of purposelessness is linked with anthropic Nothingness; the Nothingness of the end of the world, with the weakness of reality; the original and the ontological Nothingness merge, as do the solar and the thermonuclear. The confluence of these forms of Nothingness envelopes the world not only as future confluence or confluence at a distant origin. Nothingness is everywhere in the interior of the universe.

To draw a further inference, the ontological-cosmological paradox shall be referred to. Ontological Nothingness is a condition of the universe's being and survival. Even though there are currently certain strongly popularized versions of extremely complicated oriental philosophies, we can consider their essence to be the emphasis on the positivity of Nothingness. Oriental philosophies in particular try to approach the mystery of this Nothingness, which cannot be grasped or expressed in any other concept. Nothingness is not absolute Nothingness. It definitely is, even if we do not know what it is.

A further consequence is thus that, in the human spatiotemporal world of phenomena and becoming, there are operative forces that have likewise followed from Nothingness or from the annihilating primeval explosion but that nevertheless work against this scattering and destruction. These forces, which tie the organizational forms of the world back to their ecological, physical, and other conditions, are qualified by three features. First, they have a dialogic, by no means a dialectic, character. If Hegel says that unity carries dualism, duality, or contradiction within it, I would like to avoid his concept of the dialectic. Whereas the dialectic says that one is two, the dialogic says that two make one. What this means for a theory on the origin of life is that we must thus imagine substances of vastly different nature, ones such as rapidly perishable proteins that combine with less perishable or more resistant substances to produce nucleic acids. Such substances would also include one that conveys the feeling that we are living for the moment, that we are living full of pleasurable sensation, sensual pleasure, enjoyment, that we are alive, while the other would represent the principle of return, of generation, the reproduction of time, of becoming, and lastingness.

Consequently, everything being created in the universe obeys a dialogic according to which two became one, although it always remains two. This dialogic principle is also discernible in the relation between the two great concepts of order and disorder. Moreover, the self-organizing principles are always recurrent as well; they repeat; everything that reproduces itself goes in loops, returning to itself and thus becoming the agent of new production. The products, for their part, become producers of a process that produces them. It is the same processes of swirling turbulence that gave rise to the stars and that we actively encounter in the eddies of rivers as indeed in all living creatures.

The consequence pointed out here can also be linked to a hologrammatic principle according to which the whole, and thus the parts constituting the whole, always function in such a way that the whole is present within every one of its parts. The whole is based on the parts, which, in turn, are based on the whole. This is a principle *ex toto*, whereas the aforementioned principle of recurrence is *ex nihilo*, provided that *nihilo* is not understood to mean that there is nothing. After all, energies and elements are required.

The third principle mentioned, the dialogic, is a principle *ex separato*, which allows a new unit to be formed from that which is separated. This principle holds that the forces in operation clash with the Nothingness, destruction, death, and annihilation that they nevertheless harbor since they necessarily need them. From this as well there follow two paradoxical inferences. On one hand, the existing world began fifteen billion years ago; on the other, it never began. This world is heading for its end, but since it never began to exist, it can never end. From this follows a final inference. The myths that used to help exorcise death and dissipate fear are now, perhaps for the first time in the history of the human race, no longer able to ward off this fear of uncertainty, this dread of the lack of understanding and Nothingness, and the more they are confronted with the increasing strength of the forces from Nothingness, the less able they become. Apart from a self-defensive reaction by which human beings ignore negative feedback or deliberately forget and simply persist, there is an attitude of acknowledging that for the first time we are facing Nothingness in all its desolation, in all its necessity, in all its mystery. The increasing enervation of the myths, which are by no means ineffectual or dead yet, brings us for the first time to the insight that there is no messiah or also that every possible messiah is ill, not just the Messiah of religions but also that of politics. Every messiah — including that of science, including that of progress — must be told: no!

More than ever before, the need is for the anti-messiah, whose message is that there is no salvation, people cannot win, they can quit the game, they are lost. This is not a matter of intentional deception, willful disillusionment, but rather a loss of interest and enjoyment; the universe, nature, life, and thinking are nothing other than everyday life itself. Even in the life of a nothing, even in the smallest or most peculiar quirks of life an entire cosmos is revealed as soon as our Weltanschauung is freed of illusions. But despite the imbroglio of the infinite amount of information, the world has still not lost its spell, has still not been freed of illusion. In history, all promises have stemmed from the call for human brotherhood. Brotherhood was considered the guarantor of hope, the key to paradise, the gateway to the classless society. If this pythic conclusion is accepted, however, we today must base our brotherhood on our shared condition of being condemned to Nothingness. This condition is not only the foundation of what is human in the strict sense but also of brotherhood with all of life, with our cousins, the bacteria, as well as with our brothers, the animals. We live with them under the same conditions, although bacteria are far more resistant than we are. The more human we become, the more brittle, complex, and bestial we are.

If we have to play the game and are not allowed to give up in despair and disillusionment, we must elaborate a moral of lost beings, an ethic of agony that adheres to the strict sense of this ancient word: in Agon there is struggle, terrible pain, and we do not know whether it comes from growing up or from death. We are living in an agonistic time, we are members of an "agonic" species. This ethic of agony is one of the will and of thinking that certainly does not know whether it is heading for annihilation; perhaps not the annihilation of all humanity and everything that exists, but well perhaps the destruction of what we have heretofore considered to be the foundation of beauty and good, the destruction of culture, which also contains barbarism. Such an ethic of agony is at once an ethic of the end of the world *and* of the return as the new beginning of a world. This ethic requires an awareness of the end of the world, an awareness that, in all its immensity, is also moral consciousness, yes, conscience.

Dietmar Kamper

Between Simulation and Negentropy

The Fate of the Individual in Looking Back on the End of the World

1. What the title "Looking Back on the End of the World" ironically plays on is the discontinuation of a historical obsession: the end of "history" as a finite event, with a catastrophic end (and catastrophic beginning). This obsession has meanwhile become apocalyptic; it corresponds to the biography of an individual who commits suicide for fear of death.

2. The fate of the individual beyond the apocalypse would be caught between a simulated unity and a multiplicity that in cybernetic terms can be called "negentropy". That means a freedom coerced by complexity, a freedom that can generate order out of disorder and avoid catastrophe through a contemplation of the chaotic.

3. The end of the world is the end of man insofar as he is a self. Every self-contained anthropological concept tends today toward insubstantiality. The life span of man, which is linked to world eras, no longer comes to an end in just any narrative. The situation that has risen is so

open that it necessarily appears confused and bewildering at first.

4. However, the closed system can only be simulated; more precisely, only the closed system can be simulated. That is why the open situation demands a new theoretical irreconcilability that resists simulation. The acceptable alternative for the individual is to choose between autism and automation. Hidden therein is an old termination of the spirit: the imaginary death.

1. The apocalypse is a process in which something concerning the end of the world gradually becomes apparent. The apocalypse is a deferment toward better insight. The "catechon", the waiting room of history, is the place where appearances obscure and perhaps invert themselves and really bring out how the world is doing. The familiar apocalypses tell of the end of the ancient era and of the beginning of a new one. Historical accounts have retained this structure, although they have changed the outcome. Accordingly, the judgment of the living and the dead is no longer held; it becomes a permanent event: world history as judgment of the world.

Nevertheless, history continues to be determined by catastrophe. History is constantly being broken off. The relation between continuity and discontinuity is shifting in favor of breaks and leaps. Ultimately, every moment is an end, an accident, a wedge, perhaps the beginning of another life. What is profound is the vanishing of this other side. Evidently, only a "cropped" apocalypse still exists, the sense of a new world era being truncated and foreshortened.

In this sense, one must speak of the loss of eternity. The new beginning of an eon that no longer bears the terrible traits of ancient times as promised in the ancient apocalypses does not pertain today. It concerns an apocalypse without transcendence, an inherent happening that is accelerating like a cataract, losing its meaning. Thus it would be appropriate to ask whether the model of history with beginning and end has not become meaningless today. The meaning of "catechon" would then be to find that there need be no catastrophe, precisely in view of its menace. In the apocalypse would then lie the revelation that the finite event of history is only a historical obsession.

The only question that would then remain would be the source of the model's persistence. After all, it has survived the theological teachings of the history of salvation, the philosophy of world history, historiography. One is tempted to surmise that the "finite history" with catastrophic beginning and catastrophic end is linked with the greatest fear harbored by the individual and that it draws its obviousness from the birth and death of the individual human being's threatened course of life.

Recently, this fact has brought to mind that an individual who insists on one identity, accepting no split at all, falls into a strange paradox. For fear of dying, that individual chooses death. This coercive neurosis has many forms, but it is always the self that gets developed, sealed off, armored, and highly armed. As in a mirror, the image of the cropped apocalypse is repeated, a monad that is not universal, that represents no world, a windowless prison sealed off from the outer world and, perhaps, full of projection apparatuses that throw pictures of life on the walls, an embodied casing of compliance in which no thought of breaking out arises any more, an autistic neuter that, by wanting to survive, spreads deadness within and around itself.

For the will to survive is always hatching death. It

appears as if this ultimate threat enters the conscious mind nevertheless. The usual forms of public and intimate expression are full of the kind of messages in which the paradoxical pressure is involuntarily signaled. The aesthetic on the fringe of the modern spirit has a primary subject — the aforementioned fatal strategy of the individual is repeated in a mimesis of death in the hope that the reflexes for feigning death relax through reflections. Usually, however, only a stretching of catastroph comes about, a wearisome deceleration of time.

2. Suppose, then, that the millenarian and chiliastic traditions, which are deeply internalized, could be abolished shortly before the year 2000. What can one say about the fate of the individual in structural terms? Would it be possible to take stock matter-of-factly? Is there a chance beyond simulated unity, coercive, neurotic consistency, and bellicose autism?

To measure such a thing, one would have to try reversing the usual direction: variety instead of unity; "le defi de la complexité" instead of a reduction of complexity, "negentropy" instead of deadly entropy. Taking the term from cybernetic systems theory, Edgar Morin has claimed it for anthropology. "Negentropy" denotes an event that takes place in the wake of an increase in complexity, an event that forces the reinterpretation of the background and the main tendency up to that point. It does not concern a continuation in quantitative, linear series but rather a qualitative restructuration of the process itself. Morin interpreted it, along with Neumann and Günther, as the event of the "living machine". In the logic of the living, order and disorder arise simultaneously: "While the inner disorder — in the language of communication ... the 'noise', or mistake — always destroys the artificial machine, the functioning of the living machine is always accompanied by a certain 'noise' whose reliable upper limit does not decrease but rather increases as complexity increases".

From this reinterpretation of the fallacy in the direction of chance, from this switch from coercion to freedom, Edgar Morin draws the conclusion that a "different" anthropology exists. In a certain sense, there is something purely and simply paradoxical about the human being of negentropy who needs interference and distraction in order to stay alive after the increase in complexity has surpassed a certain point, who, in a novel interweaving of disorder and order, can avoid the twofold danger of deadly acceleration *and* deadly ossification, who, through the link between unconscious and conscious existence in the flow of time, anticipates the catastrophic termination of history. Thus, the slogan of the "other" anthropology is not a short-circuiting of the world, that is, not a "reduction in complexity", but rather an elimination of the entropic coercion, a refusal to act and think in closed systems.

The law of increasing entropy, according to which only those processes in a closed system spontaneously occur by which the disorder of the system increases, does not apply to the transition from complexity to hypercomplexity. That means the decline of defensive knowledge and self-knowledge. That internalized resistance to presumed overdemands that protects and arms itself in order to survive cannot be a prominent element in a strategy of negentropy. The cut-and-thrust argumentation, the defensive speech, the measures of a law court that plays up categories, the searching for the lowest common denominator, the use of signs as weapons, the entire bellicose arsenal of reason has led nowhere ever since the systematic focusing on the self, the self-referencing of thinking.

This inevitability in the liberation from coercion must be stressed once again. No one is quite prepared for it. A rousing fundamental happening that is irreversible triggers panic horror that seeks release in outmoded forms of reaction — the exclusion of chance, disorder, and the "irrational"; the use of little abstract models without regard for space and time; simplification as service to "plain common-sense"; and especially the simulation of a exclusive whole that neither matches the complex situation that should be recognized nor creates any room within the person who seeks to recognize.

3. The human being and the world cannot be equated. They do not divide evenly. The human being is not entirely a self that would be identical with the self arrived at through self-understanding. Rather, there is a difference that cannot be eliminated. That is evident in the experimental hypothesis that the world and the human being are at an end. Whoever upholds the hypothesis long enough becomes enmeshed in the illogical, that is, in that which is beside logic, aside from *doxa*, hence, becomes enmeshed in the paradoxical.

Herein lies a main motif of recent epistemological development. The demand that the recognizer find a place within his knowledge and experience makes the anthropological axioms dynamic. Self-referencing, self-focusing, self-reflection drive the question about the human being into the open. A current example of this can be cited. For some time the center of anthropological reflection has no longer been on the "animal endowed with reason" or "the rational animal", as the human being was traditionally viewed, but rather on a "self-reflective machine with imagination". Instead of the line between humans and animals, it is the transition to machines that seems to have become the main problem recently.

Although details of this shift of attention cannot be dealt with here, a glance at the epistemological consequences would be of interest. On one hand the "line", whose definition had bound nearly all efforts of anthropology for centuries, has proven progressively untenable. On the other hand – the transition to the transhuman – the propensity for "automatic self-reflection" – is linked with very highly charged expectations. The precarious machine is being ascribed with downright divine attributes. The third industrial revolution – the exteriorization of symbolization, "artificial intelligence" – carries the hope for an incomparable superiority of the great robot. It is thus not inappropriate to speak of a "deus qua machina". Naturally, one must suspect that this self-deification harbors a fallacy and that some sort of the machine's own "Fall of Man" is following close behind. More interesting, however, are the unintentional side effects of this widely installed project, to the extent that they refer back to identity and the human self. For in referring back, they are factors of a dissolution. The aforementioned transition to transhuman automation, the direction leading to a civilization without humans, has a "sliding" and "creeping" fascination. A new alienation is being produced in which technology and technocracy will become enigmatic figures to all intents and purposes. One asks oneself anew and from the outset what kind of anthropological value the devices have. Are they manifestations of power (as one had known)? Do they serve as toys, as consolations in an isolation that has long been terrifying? Do they represent the outer appearance of an irredeemable autism? Or do they mean both the end *and* the delay of the end (as one suspects)? Paul Virilio, whose writings attest to this change from the mystery of nature to the mystery of technology, speaks somewhere of a collision between counted and narrated time. It is acceleration that ends the stories in which the fate of the individual is enmeshed. That — and not reasoned discourse — leads to confusion and bewilderment. For all that, at least this much is clear — history is not structured like a biography, the biography is not structured like a story, with a beginning and an end. That was "only" the effect of narrative time, the deception that had to do with the mirror, with the priority of the imaginary in general: the heroic saga, the dramatic scenario, the novel, the apocalypse. But the director of this debacle — the imaginary death — loses its power to the extent that finiteness ceases being an essential factor.

4. In case no one manages on one hand to grasp the theory of machines, the computerization of the world, and the externalization of symbolization by humans in a different way and to expose them openly, and in case no one manages on the other hand to determine the fate of the individual negentropically, then what remains is the alternative of autism or automation, which permits no choice because it involves two impossibilities. The simulated unity, here and there, is a defensive position without a future. Manfred Frank, for example, insists on answering the question about the subject by harking back to a monadic individual that, in the model of self-reflectivity, could build on a preceding familiarity with itself. Frank once again quotes Sören Kierkegaard's protest of Hegel. The subject against which Kierkegaard turns is a radical generality; that which makes the protest is an individual. The impossibility of deceiving this individual, who, as an

individual, can neither be called a special entity (like the person) or a generality (like the subject), is tied to the "fact" of the individual's fundamental acquaintance with himself.

Such a reclaimed self-understanding is by no means natural, however, it arises from the historical production of a human nature that is datable. It may not be possible to get the better of individuality, but just as individuality originated historically, so can it be extinguished. Kierkegaard protested out of such fear. His irreconcilability has nothing to do with safeguarding but rather with the "leap" and the gamble of thinking. The model of reflexivity for which Frank makes allowances in the "original hermeneutics" of the individual is not an achievement per se but rather a calamity if one's own is only ever coupled with one's own. Namely, the older thesis of "individuum est ineffabile" means the opposite: Acquaintance, recognizability, self-knowledge as a standard figure is imputed from without. Long-term effects of the habit of identifying are involved, that is, a main variant of the body politic in the context of the process of civilization.

One could protest this by means of irreconcilability in Kierkegaard's sense: The individual remains − at the price of his vitality − unrecognizable, alien, unidentifiable for others as well as for himself. Manfred Schneider has reexamined the autobiographical text in the twentieth century and has come to results diametrically opposed to Manfred Frank's findings. All autobiography of calibre wants no familiarity with itself, no reflection, no authentic speech, no beautifully exclusive self-knowledge. Rather, it often represents an apotheosis of alienation from oneself − often against the declared intentions of the authors. Social distress presses irresistably into an incognito that ultimately can no longer be revealed. That repeats in similar veins the dynamics of the world decline already indicated, of the cataracts of history, of negentropic automation. It always involves a breach that shows a way out of the total immanence of the imaginary.

It appears that the armory of customary knowledge, the armor of the axiomatic, and the nets of closely woven communication have a weak point here — the already oft-mentioned "imaginary death". In a manner still difficult to make out, this is linked crosswise with the death of the imaginary; both are synonyms for an indescribable outside that has no reference. Within, they have the function of shielding, they conceal traumas, they constitute a writing of scars, a rebus that is a condition for writing as a rebus. It is not their meaning but rather their materiality that has recently been under discussion. There is no question but that an openness arising in such a way means a great threat to meticulous reflection and means the greatest possible seclusion for the person who writes. That seclusion may be so great that the solitary person no longer understands even himself.

Paul Virilio

The Last Vehicle

Tomorrow learning space will be just as useful
as learning to drive a car.

Wernher von Braun

In Tokyo there is a new indoor swimming pool e-
quipped with a basin of intensely undulating water in
which the swimmers remain on the same spot. The
turbulence prevents any attempt to move forward, and the
swimmers must try to advance just to hold their position.
Like a kind of home-trainer or conveyor belt on which
one moves in the direction opposite that of the belt, the
dynamics of the currents in this Japanese pool have the
sole function of making the racing swimmers struggle with
the energy passing through the space of their mutual
encounter, an energy that takes the place of the
dimensions of an Olympic pool just as the belts of the
home trainer have been replacing stadium race tracks.

The person working out in such cases thus becomes less
a moving body than an island, a pole of inertia. Like a
theater set, everything is focused on the stage, everything
occurs in the special instant of an act, an inordinate

instant offering a substitute for expanses and long stretches of time. Not so much a golf course but a video performance, not so much an oval track but a running simulator: space is no longer expanding. Inertia replaces the continual change of place.

Moreover, one observes a quite similar trend in museographic presentation. Being too vast, the most spacious exhibitions have recently been subject to temporal reduction in inverse proportion to their overall dimensions: Twice the amount of space to cover means twice as little time that one can spend at any one place.

The acceleration of the visit is measured by the area of the exhibition. Too much space, too little time, and the museum welters in useless expanse that can no longer be furnished with works of art. In any case, probably because the latter still tend to sprawl, to make a show of themselves, to pour themselves into these vast and utterly uninviting surfaces, just like the grand perspectives of classical period.

Whereas our monuments were once erected to commemorate significant works that can now be viewed for long periods by visitors interested in the past, they are presently simply ignored in the excessive zeal of the viewer, this "amateur" who seems to have to be forced to fixate for more than only a moment, for the more impressive the size of the volumes presented, the quicker he tries to escape.

We are talking about the monument of a moment in which the work tends to disappear without a trace more than expose itself. The contemporary museum vainly attempts to assemble and present these works, these pieces that one ordinarily views only from a distance in the atelier, at the workplace, in these laboratories of a heightened perception that is never the perception of the passer-by, this passing viewer distracted by his exertion. With regard to this perspective of retention, of the restriction of the time to pass through, of passing by, we should point out yet another project. It concerns a miniaturized reconstitution of the state of Israel where "in complete safety and with a minimum of physical movement, visitors can marvel at the exact copy of the Holocaust museum, a small section of the wailing wall, and the miniaturized reconstitution of the Sea of Galilee created with a few cubic meters of water from the original". Seizing this opportunity, the directors of this institution could perhaps complete it by exhibiting electronic components, products of Israeli industry. This extraterritorial manifestation could be sited in Douarnenez, on Tristan da Cunha as soon as this group of islands is finally ceded by France to the Hebrew state.

Even if this utopia does not really come to be, it nevertheless reveals in exemplary fashion this *tellurian contraction*, this sudden "overexposure" now befalling the expansion of territories, the surfaces of the vastest objects, and the nature of our latest displacement. Displacement in place, the advent of an inertia that is what has always been the "still-frame" for the film as far as the landscape through which we walk is concerned. Also the advent of a final generation of vehicles, of means of communication for distances that have nothing in common with those associated with the revolution of transport anymore — as if the conquest of space ultimately confirmed the conquest of the mere *images* of space. If in fact the end of the nineteenth century and the beginning of the twentieth experienced the advent of automotive vehicle, the dynamic vehicle of the railroad, the street, and then the air, then the end of this century seems to herald the next vehicle, the audiovisual one, a final mutation: static vehicle, substitute for the change of physical location, and extension of domestic inertia, a vehicle that ought at last to bring about the victory of sedentariness, this time an ultimate sedentariness.

The transparency of space, of the horizon of our travels, of our racing thus ought to be followed by this *cathodic transparency*, which is only the successful realization of the discovery of glass some four-thousand years ago, of iron two-thousand years ago, and that "glass showcase", that puzzling object that has constituted the history of urban architecture from the Middle Ages down to our own times or, more precisely, down to the most recent realization of this *electronic glass case*, that final horizon of travel of which the most developed model is the "flight simulator".

That is also made obvious by the latest developments in amusement parks, those laboratories of physical sensations with their slides, catapults, and centrifuges, reference models for training and flight personnel and for astronauts. In the opinion of the very people responsible, even vicarious pleasure is becoming collective experimentation with mere mental and imaginary sensations.

In the previous century the leisure park became the theater of physiological sensations to a working population for which many different physical activities had become things of the past. Thereafter, the leisure park prepared to become the scene of mere optical illusions, the place for a generalization of simulation, fictitious movements that can create in each person an electronic hallucination or frenzy − "loss of sight" following upon the loss of physical activities in the nineteenth century. Analogous to dizziness and the unusual calling of gymnasts, it is nevertheless true that the "panoramas", "dioramas", and other cinematographies smoothed the way toward the "panorama", to "Géode", a hemispheric movie anticipated by Grimoin-Sanson's "balloon cinerama". They are all old forms of our present audiovisual vehicles, whose forerunners were made more precise by the American *Hale's Tours*; after all, a few of them were actually funded by the railroad companies between 1898 and 1908. Remember that these films, which were shot on a panoramic platform either from a locomotive or from the rear of the train, were ultimately shown to the public in halls that were exact imitations of the railroad cars of that epoch. Some of these short films were made by Billy Bitzer, the future cameraman of D. W. Griffith.

At this point, however, we must return to the origins of kinematic illusion, to the Lumière brothers, to the 1895 film "L'entrée d'un train en gare de La Ciotat", and above all to the spring of 1896, when the very first traveling shot was invented by Eugène Promio.

> In Italy that I first had the idea of shooting panoramic film. When I arrived in Venice and took a boat from the train station to the hotel, on the Grand Canal, saw the banks recede from the skiff, and I thought that *if the immovable camera allowed moving objects to be reproduced, then one could perhaps also invert this statement and should try to use the mobile camera to reproduce immovable objects*. So I shot a reel of film, which I sent to Lyon with a request to hear what Louis Lumière thought of this experiment. The answer was encouraging.

To comprehend the significance of this introduction of the "mobile camera" or, to put it another way, the first static vehicle, we must again look back at the course of history. Disregarding for the moment Nadar's "aerostatic negatives" (1858), which were indeed the origin of cinematic weightlessness, one must wait until 1910 to find the first "aeronautic film", taken on board a Farman airplane. The now traditional "traveling vehicle", which was mounted on tracks and which is inseparable from the contemporary cinema, came about four years later during the shooting of *Cabiria* by Giovanni Pastrone. For memory's sake, let us also mention the trains of AGIT PROP between 1918 and 1925 and the use of train travel in the work of Dziga Vertov. He joins Moscow's film committee in the spring of 1918, waiting until 1923 in order to promote the founding of a "cinematographic automobile department" that would provide cars in emergencies if needed to film important events. The cars are thus predecessors of the mobile video productions of television. With this use of transport, this combination of the automotive and the audiovisual, our perception of the world inevitably changes. The optical and the cinematic blend. Albert Einstein's theory, subsequently to be called the special theory of relativity, appears in 1905. It will be followed about ten years later by the general theory of relativity. To make them more understandable, both take recourse to the metaphor of the train, streetcar, and elevator, vehicles of a theory of physics that owes them everything, or, as people will see, almost everything. The revolution of transport will coincide with a characteristic change of arrival, with the progressive negation of the time interval, the accelerated retention of the time of passage that separates arrival and departure. Spatial distance suddenly makes way for mere temporal distance. The longest journeys are scarcely more than mere intermissions.

But if, as already shown, the nineteenth century and a large part of the twentieth really experienced the rise of the automotive vehicle in all its forms, this mutation of it is by no means completed. As before, except now more rapidly, it will make the transition from the itinerancy of nomadic life to inertia, to the ultimate sedentariness of society.

Contrary to all appearances, the audiovisual vehicle has indeed prevailed since the 1930s with the radio, television, radar, sonar, and emerging electronic optics. First during the war, then, despite the massive development of the private car, after the war, during peace, during this "nuclear peace", which will experience the *information revolution*, the telematic informatics that are tightly linked with the various policies of military and economic deterrence. Since the decade from 1960 to 1970, what really counts does not occur through the customary communication channels of a given geographic region (hence the deregulation of rates, the deregulation of transport in general), but rather in ether, in the electronic ether of telecommunications.

From now on everything will happen without our even moving, without us even having to set out. The initially confined rise of the dynamic, at first mobile, then automotive, vehicle is suddenly followed by the generalized rise of pictures and sounds in the static vehicles of the audiovisual. Polar inertia is setting in. The second screen that can suddenly be turned on substitutes itself for the very long time intervals of displacement. After the ascendence of *distance/time* in the nineteenth century to the disadvantage of space, it is now the ascendence of the *distance/speed* of the electronic picture factories: *the statue follows upon the continual stopping and standing still.*

* * *

According to Ernst Mach, the universe is mysteriously present in all places and at all times in the world. If every mobile (or automotive) vehicle conveys a special vision, a perception of the world that is only the artefact of the speed at which it is displaced within its terrestrial, aquatic, or aerial milieu, then, vice versa, each of those visions, those optical or acoustical images of the perceived world, represents a "vehicle", a communication vector that is inseparable from the speed of its transmission. All this since the telescopic instantaneousness of the image's rectification in the passive lenses of Galileo's telescope down to our modern "means of telecommunications", our active optics of videoinformatics.

The dynamic vehicle can thus no longer be clearly distinguished from the static vehicle, the automotive no longer from the audiovisual. The recent priority of arrival over departure, over all forms of departure and, accordingly, over all forms of travel and trajectories realizes a mysterious conspiracy – inertia of the moment, of every place and every instant of the present world, which ultimately allies itself closely with the principle of inseparability, thereby completing indeterminateness in the sense meant in quantum theory.

Even when one witnesses the attempt in Japan today to combine two vehicles technologically by systematically installing video landscapes in the elevators of skyscrapers or by showing feature films during long plane flights as done in commercial air travel, this momentary link will nevertheless inevitably lead to the elimination of the least efficient vector regarding the speed of dispersion. The contemporary forward race of high-speed trains, supersonic aircraft, as well as the deregulation affecting both show better than any other preview that the threatened vector, the threatened vehicle, is really that of terrestrial, aquatic, and aerial automotility.

The era of intensive time is thus no longer that of means of physical transport. Unlike earlier, extensive time, it is solely that of telecommunications, in other words, walking in place and domestic inertia. Recent developments in both the automobile and formula-I racing prove it. Since the high performance of the audio-visual cannot seriously be improved upon, people go about altering the performance of the racing car, the rules of racing, the weight of the vehicles, and the fuel reserves. They even go so far as to reduce the power of the engines, which is really the limit! Lastly, the dynamic land vehicle and the most symptomatic one of this sporting involution is the dragster (and the hot rod), the motto of which could be "How can I get nowhere, or at least as close to it as possible (400, 200 yards), but with increasing speed?"

The extreme emphasis on this intensive competition may eventually have the finish line and starting line combined in order to pull even with the analogous feat of live television broadcasting. As far as the domestic car is concerned, its development is the same in every respect, for the automobile has a kind of self-sufficiency about it that is developing increasingly into a separate piece of property. Whence this move, this duplication of accessories, furniture, the hi-fi chain, radio telephone, telex, and videomobile that turn the means of long-haul transport into a means of transport in place, into a vehicle of ecstasy, music, and speed.

If automotive vehicles, that is, all air, land, and sea vehicles are today also less "riding animals" than *frames* in the optician's sense, then it is because the self-propelled vehicle is becoming less and less a vector of change in physical location than a means of representation, the channel for an increasingly rapid optical effect of the surrounding space. The more or less distant vision of our travels thereby gradually recedes behind the arrival at the destination, a general arrival of images, of information that henceforth stands for our constant change of location. That is why a secret correspondence between the static structural design of the residential dwelling and the medially conveyed inertia of the audiovisual vehicle becomes established with the emergence of the *intelligent dwelling* — what am I saying? — with the emergence of the intelligent and interactive city, the teleport instead of the port, instead of the train station and the international airport.

In answer to a journalist's indiscrete question about her address, a well-known actress responded: "I live everywhere!" Tomorrow, with the aesthetics and logic behind the disappearance of the architectonic, we will live everywhere, that is a promise. All of us, like the animals of the "video zoo", which are present only by virtue of a single image on a single screen, here and there, yesterday and the day before, images recorded at places of no importance, excessive suburbs of a cinematic development that finally takes audiovisual speed as it relates to the interior design of our dwellings and puts it on the same footing as what the speed of automobiles has long been for the architecture of our cities and the layout of our countries.

The "immobile simulators" will then replace the flight simulators. Behind our cathode glass cases we become teleactors and teleactresses of an animated theater whose recent developments in sound and light shows already herald this, although it is repeatedly used by people ranging from André Malraux and Léotard to Jack Lang only on the pretext of saving our monuments.

It is thus our common destiny *to become film*. Especially ever since the person responsible for the Cinéscénie du Puy-du-Fou, Philippe de Villiers, became secretary for culture and communication and announced his intent to institute "scenic walks through areas being preserved as historical sites" in order to enhance the attractiveness of our historical monuments and thereby compete with the imported "Disneyland" near Paris or "Wonderworld" near London.

In the footsteps of the theatrical scenography of the agora, forum, and church square as traditional places of urban history there now follows *cinescenography*, the sequenced mutation of a community, region, or monument in which the participating population momentarily changes into actors of a history intended to be revived. It does not matter whether it is the war in Vendée with Philippe de Villiers or the centuries-old services of the city of Lyon with Jean-Michel Jarre. Even the predecessor of the current minister of culture has paid tribute to this phenomenon by tapping the budget for funds (earmarked "Salamandar") to finance the production of an interactive videotape of a tour through the chateaus of the Loire. It is "Light and Sound" at home, and it turns the earlier visitors from a bygone age of tourism into video visitors, "tele-lovers of old stones", whose record collections and discotheques now have not only Mozart and Verdi but Cheverny and Chambord as well.

* * *

As noted in a poem entitled "La Ralentie", by Henri Michaux, "One does not dream any more; one is dreamed of, silence". The inversion begins. The film runs in reverse. Water flows back into the bottle. We walk backwards, but faster and faster. The involution leading to inertia accelerates. Up to our desire, which ossifies in the increasingly distinct medial distancing: after the whores of Amsterdam in the display windows, after the striptease of the 1950s and the peepshow of the 1970s, we have now arrived at videopornography. The list of mortal sins in the Rue Saint-Denis is confined to the names of the new image technologies like BETACAM, VHS, and VIDEO 2000 in the expectation of erotic automatism, of the vision machine.

The same is happening with military confrontation. After the home trainer for the pilots in World War I, the swivel chair for training pilots in World War II, and NASA's centrifuge for future astronauts, which is a reality test for the ability or inability to become accustomed to weightlessness, we have for ten years been witnessing the development of increasingly sophisticated and powerful simulators for the advocates of supersonic flight. Projection domes up to nine yards in diameter and more; a geode for a single man, the most developed of which will have a field of vision of up to almost three-hundred degrees because the pilot's helmet will comprise an optical system for expanding the retina. To enhance realism even more, the person who practices here will don inflatable overalls that simulate the acceleration pressure related to the earth's gravity.

The essential is yet to come, though, for tests are being run on a simulation system that is derived from the oculometer and that will finally liberate us from the spheric video screen. The presentation of the images from aerial combat will be projected directly into the pilot's eyeballs with the aid of a helmet fitted with optic fibers. This phenomenon of hallucination approaches that of drugs, meaning that this practice material denotes the future disappearance of every scene, every video screen, to the advantage of a single "seat" [siège], in this case, though, a *trap* [siège/piège] for an individual whose perception is programmed in advance by the computing capabilities of a computer's motor of inference. Before this future model of a static vehicle is invented, I think it would be appropriate to reconsider the concept of energy and the engine. Even though physicists still distinguish between two aspects of energetics - potential and kinetic energy, with the latter setting off motion − one should, eighty years after the invention of the traveling in the movies, perhaps add a third, the *kinematic* energy resulting from the effect that motion and its more or less great velocity has on ocular, optic, and optoelectronic perception.

In this sense, the contemporary industry of simulation seems like a realization of this latter energy source. The computational speed of the most recent generation of computers approximates a final type of engine: the cinematic engine.

But the essential would not yet be said if we did not return to the primacy of time over space, a primacy best expressed today by the primacy of arrival (which is momentary) over departure. If the profundity of time is greater today than that of the field, then it means that earlier notions of time have changed considerably. Here, as elsewhere, in our daily and banal life, we are in fact switching from the extensive time of history to the intensive time of momentariness without history − with the aid of contemporary technologies. These automotive, audiovisual, and informatic technologies all operate on the same restriction, the same contraction of duration. This earthly contraction questions not only the extension of the countries but also the architecture of the house and the furniture.

If time is history, then velocity is only its hallucination that ruins any expansion, extension, and any chronology. This spatial and temporal hallucination, which is the apparent result of the intensive development of cinematic energy − of which the audiovisual vehicle would be the motor today just as the mobile vehicle and, later, the

automotive vehicle were for kinetic energy yesterday —
these synthetic images, ultimately displacing the energies
of the same name that were invented in the previous
century.

Let us not trust it. The third dimension is no longer the
measure of expansion; relief, no longer the reality. From
now on the latter is concealed in the flatness of pictures,
the transferred representations. It conditions the return to
the house's state of siege, to the cadaver-like inertia of the
interactive dwelling, this residential cell that has left the
extension of the habitat behind it and whose most important piece of furniture is the *seat* [siège], the ergonomic
armchair of the handicapped's motor, and — who knows?
— the *bed*, a canopy bed for the infirm voyeur, a divan for
being dreamt of without dreaming, a bench for being cir-
culated without circulating.

Acknowledgements

The contributions to this volume stem from a symposium held in New York in the fall of 1986 with the support of the Free University of Berlin, Columbia University, the Goethe Institute and the Foundation for the Advancement of Philosophy. We are grateful to the Department of Philosophy and Social Sciences I, the Central Institute for Education and Curriculum Research and its Service Unit 3 of the Free University of Berlin for their assistance in printing this book.